Unwin Education Books: 15

WITHDRAWN

APPROACHES TO DRAMA

By the same author

The Story of the Theatre

Unwin Education Books

Series Editor: Ivor Morrish, BD, BA, DIP. ED. (London), BA (Bristol)

Unwin Education Books: 15
Series Editor: Ivor Morrish

Approaches to Drama

DAVID A. MALE

L.R.A.M. (Speech and Drama), L.R.A.M. (Mime), M. Litt.
Principal Lecturer in English and Drama Studies
Sittingbourne College of Education

London
GEORGE ALLEN AND UNWIN LTD
RUSKIN HOUSE MUSEUM STREET

Printed in Great Britain
in 10 pt Times Roman
by Cox & Wyman Ltd,
London, Fakenham and Reading

Acknowledgements

I should like to thank Christopher Parry, Stuart Bennett and David Illingworth for the articles contained in the Appendixes and the Greenwich Youth Theatre for permission to reproduce the text of their descriptive brochure.

I am most grateful to my editors, Tony Wilson and Patrick Gallagher for their constant encouragement, to my colleagues Kenneth Pickering and Irene for their help in preparing the final script and to Robert Fowler whose suggestions, and whose work with John Dick on their *English 11/16* series initiated the whole scheme. I would also like to thank Rex Walford for his helpful comments on 'Games' and simulation methods. The ideas in the book represent the interaction of experience, experiment and discussion with my colleagues, teachers, students and children and I gladly acknowledge my indebtedness to them all.

Contents

1

Dramatic Forms

INTRODUCTION

At a recent Schools' Council conference on drama in education, the delegates – teachers, lecturers, advisers – divided into discussion groups with the intention of producing, amongst other things, a definition of what was meant by drama in education. In one group it was felt necessary to define education before tackling drama and this obviously implied a lengthy process. Another group produced a statement satisfactory only to themselves, whilst a third decided to postpone the discussion until a later time. These experiences are sufficient to show that discussing approaches to drama is no simple matter. Much misunderstanding and disagreement still exists as to the nature of drama in education. Perhaps it needs to be recognised that there is no simple, clear-cut, comprehensive definition. Some kind of understanding may take place if we first make a careful examination of the main branches of drama in education and assess their individual and distinctive characteristics. With the separate activities clarified, it may then be possible to see an overall pattern if not a definition. The words 'drama' and 'education' are not happy bedfellows. The former conjures up ideas of acting and theatres, whilst the latter relates to the classroom and the learning situation. When we take a disciplined art form such as professional theatre and mix it with the free, exploratory, experiential atmosphere of a good educational drama lesson, the first may seem to be restrictive and confining. Thus it becomes essential to decide what form of drama is being attempted. Until this is settled all kinds of confusion will certainly arise. The first section of the book tries to define the main forms that drama can take and the succeeding chapters describe the characteristics of various approaches within the school situation. It cannot be emphasised too strongly that the examples quoted from time to time serve only as illustrations. They are not part of a comprehensive scheme. Though they all arise from practical experience, they are clearly inappropriate in many school situations. It is hoped that the teacher or student interested in drama will find a starting point congenial to his own attitudes and experience with the aims and objects of that approach reasonably clarified. Once confidently embarked, he may be encouraged to try other approaches so that a total experience of drama is eventually gained by the children he is teaching. Often drama is too narrowly conceived with each 'expert' or 'specialist' pursuing an individual and possibly restrictive line. The excitement of drama lies in the richness and variety of its resources. It would be tempting to compare the various approaches, but this has purposely been avoided, not through a lack of conviction, but because the job rightly belongs to the teacher. It is his job to search, test and evaluate the ideas in relationship to the children he is teaching. He will know their needs and it will be his task to enlarge and enrich their experience. A good deal of drama seems to consist of very 'thin gruel' and fails to be as exciting and involving as it might because of this sparse diet. Lessons in drama extend throughout a child's school life from infancy to near adulthood. This means that over the years a vast amount of material will be consumed and a wide variety of activities should be attempted.

A further object of the book is to introduce approaches and activities with which the teacher may be unfamiliar. Although it is claimed that too much planning will rob drama of its qualities of spontaneity and freshness, a programme of some kind must be prepared. In this way development can be observed. Classes will quickly tire of repeated ideas and the much sought-after spontaneity reduced to cliché and superficiality. Work in creative drama, improvisation, dance and play making is often less than satisfying because of a lack of resources in language, movement and experience on the part of the participants. All these areas of dramatic work should be attempted at some point. For the teacher wishing to develop a planned programme examples of two different methods are found in (i) Brian Way's ever expanding concentric approach which moves from personal discovery and mastery of personal resources towards sensitivity to others, the environment and the enrichment from inside and outside the personal environment (described in *Development through Drama*); (ii) Pemberton-Billing and Clegg's plan in *Teaching Drama* which begins with experience in movement and then passes through a series of linked activities to include speech, improvisation dance drama, etc. Neither programme may be appropriate to a particular teacher's needs, but he should be prepared to sketch out his own ideas and reasons for employing them before engaging the children's energies and emotions and using their time and intelligence in drama. Suggestions for further reading are made at the end of each section. The titles mentioned are not claimed to be exhaustive.

Drama is often described as a new subject and regarded as some kind of frill in education. Drama teachers frequently worry over justifying their work and continually question the role of drama in education. A useful reminder of the long-standing place that drama has held in schools of one kind or another will be found in Philip Coggin's *Drama in Education* which outlines the historical perspective and reveals the importance of drama in education. The book concludes with a series of detailed reports on the intentions and procedures of a range of approaches.

DRAMA AS AN ART FORM

Perhaps drama may be most easily described by reference to other forms of expression such as singing and painting which have held a traditional place in the educational curriculum for a long time. We know that the act of singing a song is a unique experience. It is not the same as looking at the words or the printed score, or hearing someone else sing. Similarly the act of painting is distinct from being told about art or looking at pictures. Both singing and painting are particular and special experiences in which the singer or painter is the essential and central participant, making his or her own contribution to the art of singing or painting. In the same way drama is a participatory activity. It is not simply being told about plays or being taken to the theatre, but an activity developed primarily from moving and speaking.

The human being's desire to sing and paint may be traced back to Man's primitive origins as cave paintings and weird aboriginal musical instruments illustrate. The desire to *move* is even more deep-rooted, not only to achieve physical aims such as walking or climbing, but also to express some inner feeling, desire or mood. In primitive societies, these expressive actions were frequently ritualised into dramatic forms of dance or mimetic magic, to demonstrate hunting techniques, evoke the aid of their gods or celebrate victory. In everyday life, we see the hands of a volatile Frenchman providing an imaginative accompaniment to his speech. The slumped, dejected look of an unemployed worker, or the lively skipping delight of a child having received a sweet or toy, indicate inner attitudes as expressively as any words. Phrases such as 'bored stiff', 'jump for joy' show the metaphoric use of physical actions or attitudes. Words may accompany these demonstrations. Language in all its richly various forms from the unequivocally direct to the whispered hint or sigh in heroic verse or contemporary slang is intimately bound up with the physical action. It is from the formalisation and disciplining of these basic elements of human physical and vocal expression that the art of drama has emerged.

In its most highly developed form this dramatic expression is converted, in Professor Reid's phrase, into the embodiment of a particular aesthetic, artistic intention. It becomes the art of *theatre* in the shape of plays, opera or ballet, performed to audiences by skilled professional artists. Sometimes this process becomes so complex that it is apparently divorced from the basic elemental form. The techniques employed by the professional actor, director and designer demand special skills in performance and presentation. The sophistication of the actual theatre building, the complexities of lighting, scenery and costume, as well as the dramatic or literary language of play combine to separate the performer from the audience to create an apparently unbreachable gulf between them. On the one hand is a skilled artist, on the other the supposedly passive, uninvolved spectator. Recent experimentation has attempted to strip away the agglomeration of theatrical devices and to reassert the simplicity of the dramatic statement being presented, to involve the audience not only as spectators but also as participants. The role of spectator does not necessarily imply passivity. Eric Bentley in *The Life of the Drama* assigns an active task to the audience:

> Events are not dramatic in themselves. Drama requires the eye of the beholder. To see drama in something is both to *perceive elements of conflict* and to *respond emotionally to these elements of conflict* (p. 4).

The audience is required to search for meaning and to respond with feeling to the demonstrated action. Whilst this task is significantly different from active participation, it is, nevertheless, not a passive role. Drama, in becoming theatre, has separated out the elements of drama into those which emphasise the doing, the imaginative involvement, the finished and polished performance; and those which require observation, receptivity and response. It has created a formalised relationship between actor and audience. Drama exists most clearly as an art form when it is in terms of theatre. It is through the theatre that the enormous and enriching greatness of the historic literary drama has been transmitted.

DRAMA AS A MEANS OF SELF-EXPRESSION

The distinction between actor and audience has no place when drama is considered as a means of self-expression and consequently, the approach will be different. Brian Way in *Development Through Drama* considers that drama in education is chiefly concerned with personal development. In distinguishing between 'theatre' and 'drama' he suggests that the major difference can be stated thus:

> 'Theatre' is largely concerned with *communication* between actors and an audience: 'drama' is largely concerned with *experience* by the participants, irrespective of any function of communication to an audience (p. 2).

With this approach, audience, actors and indeed, playwrights are assigned relatively unimportant places. The activity is 'experiential' in terms of the individual's discovery of his own self and his own potential, and its exploration in dramatic, though not theatrical, experiences of moving, speaking, responding. There is no sense of 'pretending' no demand for presentation, and no suggestion of competition in response. The criteria are created by the individual himself. Drama as self-expression aims at developing and extending personal resources not for any theatrical intention, but for individual enrichment. Although this approach seems far removed from the notion of drama as an art form, the basic 'stuff' of the two activities remains the same, i.e. the expression in physical terms of feelings, desires, needs in the world of reality or the projected world of the imagination.

The painter or musician can readily identify his instrument of expression – the paint brush or the violin that already has an objectivity of its own. The focus of attention is naturally upon the brush in contact with the paper or the bow scraping the violin string. In drama, the instrument of expression is the performer's own body and voice with all kinds of defects, skills and impulses already established. Drama as self-expression consists of the exploration and development of the particular qualities of an individual's voice and body as instruments for expressing the whole gamut of responses, thoughts, ideas, complex concepts, uncertainties that issue from that person's mind and imagination. The phrase 'tongue-tied' aptly identifies the physical blockage that prevents the vocalisation of an urgently felt desire to speak. 'All fingers and thumbs' describes another form of physical ineptness often caused by nervousness. Particularly involved with the physical and vocal skills are the senses and the imagination. It is the exploration and mastery of these resources that encourages an individual to become increasingly self-aware and to develop and enrich his own quality as a person. Drama has a particularly strong claim as the most appropriate means of encouraging this personal awareness since it relies on the response of the individual without the external focus such as a brush or music. He must become self-dependent. This process is sometimes a rather painful one with its exposure of personal doubts, failings and physical awkwardness. It can only take place in an atmosphere of sympathy and encouragement. The nature of this exposure is very different from the tensions and nervousness associated with theatrical performances or 'first night nerves'. Drama as self-expression should have a releasing and encouraging effect, though it is a great error to think of drama in terms of therapy which is a specialised, particular form best left to experts. The activity should lead to an enjoyment and understanding of the richness of individual resources. It is a self-rewarding activity rather than a means to an end.

DRAMA AS A MEANS OF COMMUNICATION

In an abbreviated form, the miniature drama of the television commercial represents drama as a means of communication. The intention of the episode is to sell the goods by inviting the viewer to join in a brief excursion into the life of an intrepid adventurer, an elegant hostess or a neighbourly housewife. The advertiser recognises the potency of drama (he often uses professional actors) in attracting the attention, absorbing interest and creating a response. But emphasis is directed towards the particular qualities of the product rather than introducing any aesthetic, artistic concern for the events or persons portrayed. Drama is being used, some claim misused, as a means of conveying an intention that is identifiably separate from the apparent, superficial intention. We are not expected to have any real concern for the person suffering from bad breath, but simply to be acquainted with the means of making our own breath sweet.

Much drama, however, is concerned with the communication of ideas, not in commercial terms, but in themes of love and hate, war and peace, or the great host of religious, political, philosophical or moralistic concepts. We are all familiar with the phrase 'a play with a message'. In this is the recognition of an intention not simply to absorb, interest or amuse, but through that absorption, interest or amusement to postulate a particular thesis. A very simple example is contained in John Galsworthy's play *Justice* which demonstrated the painful rigours of solitary confinement in prison and was successful in causing some amelioration of its harshness. More recently the television documentary, *Cathy Come Home* highlighted the problems of the homeless and succeeded in publicising their plight. Many of the greatest plays ever written adopt this approach to drama. The form is recognised as legitimately dramatic. But where the moralistic intention overwhelms the dramatic, and by violent distortion of truth or human personality the drama is subjugated to the demands of didacticism, there follows a devaluation of the art into dramatised propaganda. The description of drama as a means of communication encompasses an immense bulk of dramatic fare ranging from scripted plays to television documentaries. It is the area in which there is considerable discord and argument and therefore represents a dangerous, though highly exciting, approach to drama.

USE OF THE WORD 'DRAMATIC'

A number of words have been introduced into the preceding summary that need more precise definition. Among them, 'dramatic' and 'aesthetic' particularly require clearer terms of reference. Firstly we must recognise that 'dramatic' does not necessarily connect with drama. The adjective is a favourite for newspaper headlines when some exciting, highly toned word is required. To announce a 'dramatic' revelation is usually to disclose some scandalous or shocking proceeding. Many games of sport include highly 'dramatic' incidents – goals, fouls, fisticuffs, and the child psychologist will talk of 'dramatic' play. This is not to suggest that the word is being incorrectly used, but that the connection with drama is co-incidental. Drama has its own forms, disciplines and characteristics that separate it from games and newspaper reports, though indeed it may well make use of any of the incidents just described. Drama is not simply 'a slice of life'. That, as Eric Bentley reminds us, is the raw material of the plot. In creating a play, the material has to be modified, shaped, given dialogue and location, i.e. *objectified* by the conscious intention of the constructor, i.e. the playwright. He may use traditional means of shaping and modification that have respect for historical formulae for play construction postulated from Aristotle onwards, or he may invent new, unfamiliar and challenging forms that extend the art into a new dimension. The 'dramatic' becomes drama when it is re-created by the artist. In a play, the process involves playwright, actor, director; in ballet, the choreographer, the dancer, the musician. The re-creative vitality contained in the actor's or dancer's physical skill, sensitivity and imagination is the means by which the slice of life becomes art.

USE OF THE WORD 'AESTHETIC'

To attempt a simple explanation of 'aesthetic' is to invite disaster. Philosophers such as Susanne Langer, Herbert Read or Louis Arnaud Reid treat this matter in considerable depth and reveal its immense complexities. But perhaps it can be suggested at least, that in using the word 'aesthetic' we express a concern for and response to the qualities of beauty, form, shapeliness, wonder, excitement that are contained within an object as an integral part of its existence whether it is a painting, sculpture, poem, dance or play. Notions of what is aesthetically pleasing develop from past experience and present experiment related to the particular art. Responses and tastes change, so that the description of aesthetic as applied to a particular artifact may change. Traditionalists will assert that fairly firm rules have emerged, but these are by no means universally accepted. Here is another area of argument which will certainly affect one's approach to drama.

This introductory summary is intended as a survey of some of the different forms in which drama appears. It is important to recognise that the categories are not mutually exclusive. A good deal of unnecessary antagonism and difficulties occur amongst teachers of drama when they denigrate or simply disregard ways other than their own. The intention in the ensuing chapters is to examine the characteristics of a number of approaches to drama without attempting too many value-judgements.

Introductory reading on the subject of drama in education is likely to lead the reader into very deep waters. It must be remembered that drama is not a superficial, frivolous subject. It is supported on historical, philosophical, theoretical and practical grounds. Richard Courtney's *Play, Drama and Thought* is an examination of the intellectual background of drama in education and an earlier publication, *Drama in Education* by A. F. Alington includes a helpful general survey. Philip Coggin's *Drama in Education* supplies a historical perspective, whilst Caldwell Cook's *The Play Way* prefigures many modern developments. Brian Way's *Development through Drama* and Peter Slade's *Introduction to Child Drama* are the fruit of years of practical experience. They contain many useful ideas and examples of educational drama in practice. *Drama and Theatre in Education* edited by Nigel Dodd and Winifred Hickson is a collection of papers first presented at a Bristol Conference in 1969. Contributions by Gavin Bolton on 'Drama and Theatre in Education: A Survey' and by Dorothy Heathcote on 'Drama in Education: Subject or System' comment on the relationship between drama and theatre and the educational concepts involved.

Eric Bentley's *The Life of Drama* is a skilful and informative analysis of drama and dramatic modes. At a philosophic level, Louis Arnaud Reid's *Meaning in the Arts* and Herbert Read's *The Meaning of Art* consider the nature of art and aesthetics. Susanne Langer's *Feeling and Form*, whilst primarily concerned with the philosophy of Art, makes many comments that are apposite to the visual elements of drama. In *Play, Dreams and Imitation in Childhood* Jean Piaget draws on his experience with young children to formulate theories of behaviour and role play which connect directly with drama.

Readers who find the foregoing list rather daunting might like to look at the section in the Bibliography entitled 'Techniques and Approaches'. This includes a number of writers who discuss general theories before outlining or discussing individual approaches.

2

Drama in the Curriculum

The word drama may appear on a school time-table under any number of pseudonyms and in many different guises. The label may indicate a voluntary recreational group meeting after school hours such as Wiles and Garrard describe in *Leap to Life*, or simply refer to a series of school radio or television broadcasts. It can identify a particular and regular series of lessons undertaken by a specialist teacher, or be part of a creative arts programme. One school, considered a new model for secondary education has on its time-table 'Creative and expressive work in words, music and movement'. This programme includes music, physical education, drama, dancing and English. For younger children, drama as such may play a relatively small part in the general scheme undertaken by a non-specialist teacher. Drama can exist in its own right or in association with other subjects, or at worst, in name only, having been squeezed out of existence by an over-demanding time-table, an unenthusiastic teacher or apparently unresponsive children.

According to the particular role that drama is expected to fulfil so its form and content must be appropriate. A good deal of misunderstanding, even chaos, arises from the teacher's failure to recognise exactly what he wants to do either through lack of information, inexperience or perhaps a wrong approach. Many books on the teaching of drama, though excellent records of marvellously creative individual attitudes full of useful suggestions, lack an introduction that identifies their underlying aim, assuming that the mere description of the content of the drama lesson will imply its intention. Unfortunately this is not always the case. These books, contrary to their authors' intentions, may provide pitfalls for the unwary who only partially understand the intentions, misapply the suggestions and, dispirited by the ensuing chaos, give up. Some authors are perhaps aggressively over-insistent on a particular approach. Brian Way's suggestion that the teacher should be free to 'approach the matter from where he or she feels happiest and most confident' is a valuable one. It is essential to venture out of calm, well-charted harbours to the more demanding deeps, but not before experience and success 'inshore'. The sections and chapters that follow attempt to examine the many facets of educational drama so that the teacher is able to appreciate the objectives, find a starting-point or extend an

B

interest. It is important to have long-term aims, so that a balanced scheme can be planned. Sustained and deep interest in one aspect of drama temporarily at the cost of neglecting others is perfectly acceptable, provided that, in time, the other aspects come back into focus. Programmes at all age levels should be thought of in terms and years rather than weeks. The time allotted may vary from a single brief period to several hours per week. It is possible for effective work to be accomplished in short as well as long spans of time. The work, however, will be substantially different in approach and intention according to the time available. Broadly speaking, a teacher must assess his resources in terms of time and frequency of lessons, availability of space and equipment, relationship with other activities, his own teaching strength, where he can seek help and, of course most importantly, the children who are being taught. Only then is it possible to devise an effective plan for drama in the curriculum. Dependence upon inclination, chance or fortuity is not enough.

DRAMATIC PLAY

Any observer seeing an individual child or group of youngsters involved in physical activity would readily describe the activity as 'play'. Investigation of the nature of this play has revealed that, far from being a frivolous, time-wasting activity, it is a serious, absorbing and educating process. One famous investigator of children's play in terms of physical activity and language is J. Piaget. He shows that children's play activity operates in two ways, one concerned with experiment in physical activity, e.g. the delight of jumping over a rope, or standing on one's head, and the other, an activity involving the imagination where the immediate physical objective is less important than the imagined object or person with whom the child is engaging himself. It may be described in such terms as 'make-believe' or 'pretend', but this does not imply a superficial, artificial activity. Those simple phrases describe an activity of the imagination which allows action to be translated, developed or interpreted in ways different from the immediate and obvious. Piaget calls this play symbolic. It is the basis of all drama. For many years this activity has been approved of as suitable for infants, but neglected with rather older children. More recently the term 'role play' has been introduced to describe quite sophisticated dramatic and non-dramatic activities. What is implied in that activity is the use of symbolic play as defined by Piaget. Role play is used in exploratory and problem-solving situations where conjectures and responses are worked out, not in terms of objective discussions but in an active participatory manner, with those involved taking on the roles demanded by the situation, and coming to terms with those persons and their attitudes. Symbolic play is a serious and deeply felt process even if it is described as 'play'. Through symbolic play we can experience the projection of ourselves as other persons, responding freely, sometimes unrestrainedly to feelings, emotions, ideas that we might normally, consciously keep in check. Symbolic play, however, can be terminated. We return to our normal selves enriched, extended perhaps even a little sobered by the exploration.

It is worth noting some of the characteristics of this dramatic play; (i) it involves the imagination; (ii) usually some element of impersonation is present; (iii) feelings and emotions are engaged; (iv) it is an activity consciously embarked on and relinquished; (v) it is a means by which we can extend our experience and examine our relationships with the environment and other people, 'coming to terms with the world'.

A typical example of dramatic play is observed in the vicinity of a 'Wendy' house or similar construction in an infant classroom. This make-believe environment provides a miniature of the world known to the child and the familiar processes of life are enacted – eating, cooking, washing, sleeping, receiving visitors, gossiping and the more special events such as christenings, marriages and funerals or visits by doctors and nurses. A child might deliberately select a particular role and use the opportunity to give expression to submerged, half-conscious desires that the play allows. Another similar focus is the 'dressing up' box containing a variety of materials, hats, shoes, scarves, beads, belts, coats, etc., which stimulate play. *Drama Survey* (p. 7) notes a tendency for the play corner to be 'excessively domestic'. To guard against this, more specialised objects, crowns, wands, masks, tinsel, barrows, carts, hobby horses and shop fronts might be included to invite a wider range of imaginative activities. More important are objects that do not immediately identify themselves, but allow imaginative use, such as portable blocks, corrugated cardboard, empty cartons, tubes, containers and lengths of material. The play corner will be one of a number of activities going on in the classroom. It is unlikely to be called drama and the children's activity should not be described as acting but as dramatic play. This play may be individual or in small, often changing groups, brief in duration. It may well be of no interest to other children engaged in other activities – nor should it be. It is inadvisable to cultivate a sense of performing to an audience. Dramatic play is personal and exploratory and should not be made into demonstrated drama. The teacher is simply providing an environment in which symbolic play may most easily take place. The objects present stimuli to be utilised or rejected. The everyday items provide an opportunity to explore the familiar world and the more exotic items allow the exploration of stories, rhymes, poems or jingles and pictures which are part of the world of language, literature and art. Various items may be used by the children in a number of unusual and highly individual ways. Attempts to establish a rigidly conventional use of the materials should be avoided.

What is the teacher's role in dramatic play? She should ensure an adequate provision of stimulating materials and allow ample opportunity for them to be used. Her most important job is that of observation; noticing (i) what objects attract particular attention and the imaginative use to which they are put; (ii) the responsiveness and involvement of the children at play – problems and difficulties may be revealed which at the appropriate moment may be sympathetically handled; (iii) what incidents or stories are selected for symbolic play and conversely, occasionally using one of the objects as a focus for a story or a poem or in the narration of an everyday incident.

The teacher must never lose sight of the fundamental intention of dramatic play by allowing it to be teacher-directed, superficial, contrived, or overlaid with conventional adult values that might destroy individual, personal responsiveness. Excessive praise or criticism by the teacher has no place. The need is for a quiet sense of interest and a readiness to enter the imagined world that the play symbolises.

Games

Peter Opie's exploration in *Lore and Language of Schoolchildren* has revealed a very rich vein of information concerning children's games. At an earlier period in our history, the medieval tournament with all the trappings of heraldic shields, beautiful princesses and knightly gallantry was, in fact, a development using dramatic devices of the very serious business of battle training needed by the medieval warrior for survival. The sword fighting, tilting and jousting was organised into a rather complicated contest or game that elevated the harsh training into a more enjoyable activity. The organisation and the competition gave shape to a physical activity. In a simple way the game of hop-scotch is an organised competitive development of the action of hopping. Numerous children's games have similar origins. Opie's book is a revealing commentary upon the richness of the 'game' world. It is different from dramatic play yet it utilises certain features which are common to both activities. There has to be some co-operation and agreement on the roles to be played – who is to be chaser, how points have to be scored. The very names of the activities and the participants (e.g. Blind Man's Buff, medievally known as Hoodman's Blind and played by the soldiers in 'The Buffeting' sequence of the Wakefield Mystery Cycle) indicate the presence of some kind of symbolism which shows affinities with dramatic play. The main difference lies in the absence of competition in dramatic play and this difference needs to be maintained.

The experience gained from dramatic play and participation in games provides the child with a means of identifying and testing himself, impersonating others, extending actual and imaginative experience in physical activity and language and in learning to co-operate within a group. It is based upon an instinctive human desire to give verbal and physical expression to thoughts, ideas and even fantasies. It is an activity with a deep sense of personal control and involvement and is anything but childish.

This activity is so important that it should not be confined to the infant classroom. The basic need still requires satisfaction as the child grows through the junior into the secondary school and adulthood. The name of the activity may change to 'Improvisation', 'Role Play' or 'Management Games', but it remains fundamentally dramatic play and as such must be handled seriously and sympathetically.

Dramatic play is a very necessary preparation for child drama which utilises the experiences gained and develops them as the child grows in skill, experience and sophistication.

Some teachers feel that their provision of stimuli in materials, stories and suggested activities is a form of imposition preventing the emergence of the children's own responses and ideas. The imposition does not, in fact, come from the materials, but rather from an insistence upon their particular use or an unwillingness to allow their rejection. The environment of the classroom should be an enriching one suggesting possibilities and inviting exploration. The child's struggle to come to terms with himself and the world should not go unaided. What must be avoided is rigid structuring, imposition of adult standards and restricting of responses.

INFANT DRAMA

The question may be asked at this point whether infant drama is synonymous with dramatic play. To a large extent it is, but during the course of the child's infant school career the emphasis may change so that an activity that more resembles drama than play emerges. The whole point of dramatic play is that it is unencumbered by structure, that it provides an opportunity for the child to give expression to his thoughts, feelings and ideas in a symbolished form. His play can move rapidly from one context to another, his role can vary equally quickly. He may play by himself or briefly engage with others. But the initiative for activity lies with the child. The focus of dramatic play may be on a number of diversified objects such as a Wendy house, play blocks, dressing-up clothes or relate to a particular construction that has been built by a group of children, such as a castle, airport or encampment.

Perhaps the chief developments that will gradually emerge are (i) the extension of the imaginative situations; (ii) a sense of patterning in the activity and the utilisation of the space; (iii) the introduction of stories that have a strong dramatic shape in terms of plot and incident; (iv) the sustaining of roles and improvisation within the role over slightly longer periods. Activities in painting and music-making provide parallel examples of development. The process will certainly extend over two to three years and should not replace dramatic play. Rather should it be an extension or adjunct.

This period is vital in the development of a child's sensitivity and awareness. He has come to terms with physical activities such as walking and speaking. He is gaining dexterity in handling objects – knives and forks, pencils, brushes, balls, bricks. He is becoming skilful in painting, singing games, music making and in listening to stories and poems. The process of reading, with all the delights that it promises, is becoming a distinct possibility if not already attained. There is a liveliness in physical and imaginative responses and a readiness to be involved and enjoy. The teacher must take advantage of this readiness by offering a rich diet of stories, poems, rhymes and songs, and by physical activities that use symbolic play in group situations where a sense of co-operation may just be beginning to emerge. The children should acquire a store of stories, rhymes and jingles to which they can refer or develop in dramatic terms. Their vocabulary should be enlarged by words which emphasise the sound attributes, the colourful metaphor or the apt description and the children should be encouraged to use these newly acquired words in active situations.

So far as the space is concerned, the need for structure and pattern may become more necessary. In dramatic play the same object may be fulfilling a number of identities simultaneously – for one child, a palace, for another a mountain hut – but in group work, agreement will be necessary and the construction of the particular environment may well be part of the activity. The surrounding space then becomes identified more clearly and what Ron James in *Infant Drama* calls a 'ground plan' will develop.

The types of stories selected for use in dramatic work will be those that have a sense of development in terms of a plot or series of episodes, vividly characterised personalities and a feeling of excitement, suspense and climax. The hero may undertake a series of tasks each of which requires the overcoming of a particular obstacle or adversary using a variety of skills (e.g. the labours of Hercules). Teachers need to exercise their skill and sensitivity by selecting material that will lead to the enrichment of the children's imagination rather than by reiterating cliché-ridden stories of third rate standards. Of course, stimuli other than stories may be used, music, sound effects, costumes, properties such as carved boxes, silk scarves, masks, objects brought home from holidays abroad, anything that suggests far-away people, outlandish places or exciting colours and textures. The structuring of the activity is simply to provide a framework for exploration and should not be constricting. One need not stick rigidly to a story or use all of it. The children should be encouraged to suggest variations but these should be taken up in action rather than in discussion. A word of warning needs to be sounded at this point. The dramatic activity is *not* a performance. The space should be arranged for the convenience of the participators. Ordinarily there would be no spectators. All the children should have an opportunity to explore the main characters. There should be no early selection of the 'best actors' for the 'best parts'. If necessary several groups should operate at the same time so that there is maximum involvement.

In this work in infant drama, three elements can be distinguished: (i) doing, (ii) characterisation or role playing, (iii) patterning. Doing is principally concerned with the activity – climbing, searching, digging and all will participate. Teachers with a special interest in movement will consider the notions of movement and stillness, locomotion, body and space awareness. For others a more mimetic emphasis will be more appropriate. Ideally both should be combined. Who is 'doing' is the next question. The child may invent a character for himself or respond to a suggestion contained in the story or poem that has been introduced as the basis for drama. All the children should interpret freely. No rigidly precise instructions should be issued. When the characters and the situations have been explored, then some kind of dramatic shaping or patterning may evolve. This need not include the whole of the story that was the original stimulus, neither should the plot be slavishly adhered to. Indeed the teacher may simply use the opening of the story and allow the invention to proceed from the children. A few properties or blocks may be used, but nothing should in any way inhibit free movement. Cloaks and hats that have to be clutched to prevent their slipping off do nothing to help the drama. What is worn should be firmly attached and allow unimpeded body and arm movement.

This readiness of infants to respond may sometimes be taken advantage of by teachers who train their pupils in puppet-like action patterns that have a superficial attractiveness but, in fact, are very firmly imposed. Some 'action' songs or scripted plays fall into this category. They should be used warily and sparingly – if at all.

In a brief but apt introduction to *Infant Drama*, Ron James makes some helpful comments on the approach to infant work and the examples in the book show what a wide variety of stories can be attempted. Janet Goodrich's *Drama in the Primary School* includes a useful analysis of the movement and language characteristics of children at different ages with suggestions for appropriate dramatic work. The *Teacher's Notes* and pamphlets for the BBC *Movement and Music, Stages I and II* and *Movement, Mime and Music, Stage I* are also good sources of suggestions, procedures and materials even if, for some reason, the broadcasts are not used. Laban's Themes and other work in movement are discussed in Joan Russell's *Modern Dance in Education* and *Creative Dance in the Primary School*.

For the literary approach a most illuminating book is Elizabeth Cook's *The Ordinary and the Fabulous* which distinguishes between the forms of fable, myth and legend and makes helpful assessments of translations and simplified versions. Diana Jordan's *Childhood and Movement*, Vera Gray and Rachel Percival's *Music, Movement and Mime for Children* and Esme Woodland's *Poems for Movement* will supply detailed information and discussion on particular approaches and methods.

PHYSICAL EDUCATION

The body that in drama is the chief instrument of expression, is the same one that plays hop-scotch, badminton or swims the butterfly stroke. The body that crouches in preparation for the hundred metre sprint is the same one that may crouch in fear of an imaginary assailant. Whilst the instrument of physical and dramatic activity remains constant, the intention and the objectives alter. Another constant is the presence of inner feeling in response to physical activity. It would be a stony athlete who, successful in his endeavours, did not experience some sense of tension, elation or burst of feeling, perhaps not outwardly demonstrated, but observable in the quick pulse, the narrowing eye, the gritted teeth.

The body is used for both physical activity and the demonstration of feelings and emotional stakes. The dejected attitude of the unemployed worker is plain enough. A cricketer going through the process of bowling an inswinger uses his body in both ways: first in the complex technicalities of the run-up and the finger grip and then in expressing his delight or disappointment with the delivery. We are well aware of the physical demonstrations that accompany the appeal for a catch or a stumping.

There is a good deal of drama or, rather, a sense of the dramatic in the most exciting football match or a tedious cricket draw. As well as the application of physical prowess, there is the conflict – sometimes actual fisticuffs – between teams, individual duels of guile, the climax of goal, penalty, stumping or century, the embrace of victors, the tears of the defeated. The whole activity is performed within a pattern similar in many ways to a play. Of course it is not drama, but the carefully selected and refined physical actions and emotional responses are not unlike drama. Time and time again, newspapers print action shots which reveal the beauty and elegance of body control of the swerving forward or the leaping goalkeeper. It would be surprising if the players admitted a deliberate aesthetic intention. The potentiality for beauty or expressiveness, strength, delicacy in movement is what is made conscious in drama. One or two excursions have been made by footballers and tennis players into ballet techniques as part of their training without much success. The inclusion of decorative gestures in gymnastic sequences are often superficial. There is however a dynamic relationship between *physical education* and *drama* particularly in *movement and dance*. Each involves physical agility, sensory awareness and emotional sensitivity to a greater or less degree. In P.E. the objective may dominate – to jump the five-foot bar; in movement, the concern is with the body shape, its pathway on the ground and in the air; dramatically, the feelings, the tensions, the emotional content will be the decisive factor.

Awareness in terms of the body's movement possibilities is basically important. The ability to stretch, curl and twist, to travel and stop involves elements of energy or force, management of weight, awareness of space occupied or explored and the time and speed involved. In table-tennis, the need for quick deft movements is obvious. Equally speed and deftness might be the physical characteristics of a particular character in drama. For example, the character of Harlequin in the *Commedia dell 'Arte* has precisely these qualities. Physically speaking, the individual movement style of a particular person consists of a combination of his body shape, his space awareness and mode of travelling. The two table-tennis players also show a preoccupation with space, not only in relationship to each other, but to the table and the floor. They crouch, reach, turn and spin in an elaborate floor and air pattern attempting to outwit their opponent. All kinds of devices of speed, suddenness, unexpected changes in rhythm and pattern are employed. The players both compete and co-operate in abiding by a particular set of agreed rules. In *movement* and *dance* the spatial concern is expressed in terms of floor and air patterns and the organisation of bodies in the space, perhaps with some kind of musical or rhythmic accompaniment. In drama, this physical action and spatial patterning is likely to be related to a particular situation or environment. It will involve imaginative exploration of expressive possibilities in terms of character and feelings. All these activities are developments and refinements of ordinary, everyday human movement.

Before considering the part that movement plays in both physical education and drama, it is worth observing that certain physical activities have a direct relationship. Many dramatic improvisations and plays call for precise athletic skills. Shakespeare's plays, for example, include fencing, sword and dagger fights, wrestling, battles with staves, clubs, lances and bouts of fisticuffs. Comedy may ask for acrobatic expertise, tumbling, balancing, leaping, climbing. Period plays may call for competence in dancing. Military situations frequently require various kinds of marching and weapon handling. All these activities demand physical agility with some knowledge of the particular art of fencing, sabre fighting, boxing, wrestling, foot drill, self-defence or acrobatics. Some are potentially dangerous. In all, practice in falling, weight management and footwork is important. The brilliant 'coke stealing' episode in Wesker's *Chips with*

Everything depends for its effectiveness on a combination of physical dexterity, timing and group awareness. Fights may vary from the blood-thirsty encounter between Macbeth and Macduff to the confrontation of the mutually frightened Andrew Aguecheek and Viola in *Twelfth Night*. In drama, of course, the bouts usually have a pre-arranged conclusion and avoid the intention of actually killing or maiming. William Hobbs's *Techniques of the Stage Fight*, which is a mine of valuable information, lists many examples of accidental injury and suggests very positive safety precautions. Some skill will obviously be beneficial. It is vital that the 'as if' element of drama is fully understood so that the most violent stage opponents learn the need for careful co-operation. Brian Way devotes a chapter of *Development through Drama* to 'Fighting and Violence'. Facility in dancing and marching becomes important when period dances or military drills are required on the stage. It is surprising how often they are called for. The ability to move rhythmically for the quadrille or the slow march will be important in the scene where it is required. Poorly executed fighting or shoddy ill-timed dancing will certainly reduce the dramatic effectiveness. The final scenes of *Hamlet* call for skill in fencing, falling, lifting and carrying and marching, all of which must be dextrously performed if the play is to reach its final solemn conclusion. A full analysis of the *Hamlet* duel will be found in Arthur Wise's *Weapons in the Theatre*. This book illustrates the armoury of weapons involved in stage fighting and gives detailed advice on the mechanics and requirements of particular historical periods. Lyn Oxenford's *Playing Period Plays* gives help with period movement, dances, bows and curtsies. In talking about his play *Sergeant Musgrave's Dance*, John Arden commented that part of its initial impetus lay in his fascination with an old army drill book of his father's. This play, incidentally, requires the actors to handle rifles and a machine-gun, manipulate ammunition boxes; march, parody military drill; fight with fists, clubs, tankards, bayonets; perform clog dances and die violent deaths. Peter Brooks's production of *A Midsummer Night's Dream*, influenced by a Chinese Circus performance in Paris, demanded that the performers executed cartwheels, somersaults, swung on trapezes, climbed ladders and ropes, juggled, and generally behaved in a lively athletic style. John Kane, who played the part of Puck wrote in *Flourish*, the Royal Shakespeare Company newspaper:

The next morning we began the physical training to prepare for the demands the acting style was to make of us. Every morning began with a 'warm-up' session accompanied by an extended version of the improvised drumbreak which opens the second half of our performance. Over the eight week rehearsal period, the Studio filled with trapezes, ropes, plastic rods, spinning plates, tennis balls, hoops, paper, string and a variety of musical instruments. For at least half an hour everyday we exercised with these until they became extensions of ourselves.

These examples should be sufficient to illustrate an important feature of drama that is closely related to physical skill, strength and dexterity and to indicate what a valuable contribution it has to make. One must not, however, overstress the overlap, important and exciting though it is. What really unifies *drama* and *physical education* is their common concern with *movement* in all its aspects.

MOVEMENT AND IMPROVISATION

Part of the physical activity of a growing baby lies in the exploration of what movements its body is capable of performing. The constant flexing of fingers and stretching of limbs, the lift of the head and the struggle to crawl, stand and walk are examples of attempts to master the body and utilise its functions for initially such simple tasks as grasping a cup, or much later to perform the complicated action of the butterfly swimming stroke. The objective may vary from the simple delight of just doing an action to a specific occupational intention, or the physical expression of some inner feeling. The clasping and unclasping of the fist may be used to grab a sweet, but it can also indicate the existence of an inner nervous tension.

The basic actions of which the body is capable are bending, stretching and twisting, either as a whole or in a particular part. An analysis of these movements suggests that a number of factors combine to produce a particular movement. Briefly, in simplified terms they are: (i) the degree of energy required to achieve an action, ranging from a great deal of force to the finest and most delicate touch; (ii) the time it takes to accomplish the action which again may extend from the extremely slow to the sudden, instantaneous. Also involved is (iii) the direction that the action takes in space. It might be straight and undeviating or alternatively, roundabout, indirect with all the variations between those two extremes. By including a consideration of (iv) how easily the action is stopped, these factors allow a fairly precise description of nearly all human action. Of importance to us is the fact that by varying one of these factors of force, space, speed or control, movements of substantially different quality are produced. For example, a quick direct strong arm movement is easily identified as a punch, a 'straight left', but by simply reducing the speed of that punch whilst leaving the other factors unaltered, the punch becomes a press, useful, but not so effective to the boxer. Experiment with these basic actions will introduce us to a wide range of physical activities in which we can explore the effects and applications of different combinations.

Direction involves shape and space. Each person occupies a certain volume of space by virtue of his own body shape and he can also explore the space surrounding him upwards, downwards and outwards. This spatial dimension greatly increases movement possibilities. The number of people involved (pairs, trios, and larger groups) also increases the variety of activities. In summary, the movement equipment that everyone possesses consists of his own body and the actions he can initiate, either by himself or in relation to other people in some kind of space.

Movement with all its ramifications supplies the physical expressiveness that the actor seeks. Certain basic elements possess an inherently dramatic quality that is important to recognise. For example: one of the most fundamental dramatic qualities is contained in the contrast between movement and stillness. Such vivid expressions as 'rooted to the spot', 'still as the grave', 'greased lightning' show an immediate dramatic meaningfulness in motionlessness or rapidity. Within the simple physical action of stopping, the range of variations is considerable. The speed of the movement can be changed, the readiness with which the stop is achieved, the length of the pause or temporary stop, the speed of the resumption of movement. Each of these changes can make a fresh and different dramatic statement. Phrases such as 'Hold it', 'Pause for a moment', 'On your marks, get set, go!' illustrate the dynamism of the 'still/moving' contrast. But behind those expressions lies a further question. Why must we 'hold it'? Why must we 'pause for a moment'? Implied is some kind of a reason or motive. An abrupt halt and a gradual deceleration differ only in the speed with which they are accomplished, but they invite very different interpretations. We conjecture the reason, we search for the motivation. It is sometimes useful to investigate the physical task of moving and stopping before considering motive. The task itself will often induce an imaginative response from the performer and prevents a stock response to a supposedly exciting stimulus. In the demand for the sudden stop, the pupil can often invent a variety of different motives or situations not even considered by the teacher. The sudden stop can be a response to the challenge 'Halt! Who goes there?', avoiding a speeding car; the slower stop may be a faint following a wearisome journey, or the gradual recollection of something left behind at home. Also fundamentally dramatic is a change in level such as a rise or fall. Solving the technical problem of falling without hurting oneself is a useful experience. It may well provide a good starting point. Falling can happen quickly as a result of a blow, a shot, a trip; or more slowly as in sinking to the knees, or fainting. The Duel scene in *Hamlet* illustrates an interesting diversity of falls – the rapier cuts, the retrieval of a dropped foil, Gertrude's poisoned drink, the violent attack on Claudius, the dying Laertes and Hamlet. Rising is associated with ideas of ascent, climbing, reaching, imploring, or aspiration and hope, very different from the 'sinking' feeling of despair and hopelessness. An investigation of the possibilities contained in rising and falling can give rise to many dramatic situations. The climax of a situation is frequently in a rise or fall.

Except for a small group of monodramas almost all play plots can be described as a series of meetings and partings. By and large, we can describe a play as a coming together, a reaction to the meeting, then a development in some kind of separation and a resolution in permanent divorce or unity. Inevitably the coming and going poses the question of motivation. All kinds of variations on this theme are possible. One person meets a large group, two individuals confront each other. The first dramatic moment arrives in the initial recognition. From that moment an actual meeting becomes a definite possibility. The decision to persist or desist from meeting remains open. The meeting may develop into an embrace or combat. Alternatively there might be a retreat, avoiding direct confrontation. All the alternatives invite different motivations. Dramatic literature is full of examples revealing the particular exciting dramatic quality inherent in meeting and parting. Romeo and Juliet, Hamlet and the Ghost quickly come to mind. By varying the speed of an action a number of different situations can be created. Slowness might be accounted for by a physical limitation such as a limp or injury, or enforced by the hazards over a snow-covered, muddy terrain. It is important always to encourage the freest possible exploration of a particular action so that the participant's imagination is actively engaged rather than his simply performing a mimetic instruction. Even the shape the performer adopts with his body has dramatic potential. A hunched position suggests feelings of secrecy, withdrawal or protection. In this case the limbs and body are close together. Conversely the open, stretched position gives a sense of striving, imploring, reaching outwards, stretching. Opportunity should be taken to explore the dramatic possibilities inherent in body shape. Suppose in a room we see a number of bodies lying on the floor, some are hunched, others flat, or spreadeagled on the floor. From their attitudes we would attempt to infer a particular situation. Maybe they are sleepers in a dormitory, or sunbathers on a beach, or a group of dead and dying soldiers. In everyday life we are quick to see and to respond to body shapes as they indicate particular attitudes; cringing fear, defiant stiffness, the drooped shoulders of the depressed. It is important to stress in all these physical activities that no set or conventional formulae are implied. We must not make the mistake of equating, too specifically, action and emotion. Imaginative exploration of the actions is necessary to find out *all* their dramatic possibilities. A nineteenth-century book on acting gives a very detailed explanation of the physical requirements for the demonstration of rage on the stage. They include bared teeth, drawn back lips, clenched fists and a stamping foot. This kind of directive is to be avoided. Very often the same action will evoke a whole range of responses. What is important is to discover and extend that range.

All the activity discussed so far has had a conclusion in some kind of improvised drama related to a particular set of movement patterns. Improvisation has both physical and vocal aspects which should not be thought of apart, but for convenience are discussed separately. Improvisation is a response in physical and verbal terms, initiated by the desire to achieve an action, express some thought or idea or indicate a mood. Any physical or vocal limitation is likely to reduce the range of responsiveness. Vocally, for example, if the total vocabulary amounts to only a few words, they, together with a few grunts, shouts or screams, constitute the complete range of expression available to that speaker. A wider vocabulary allows a more varied and precise response. The same argument applies in the physical aspects. At its most perfect, the professional mime, such as Marcel Marceau, reveals expressive control over the tiniest movement which he uses with the utmost subtlety.

Perhaps we need to define what is meant by improvisation. As an activity it has attracted a great deal of attention in recent years. It has acquired most vigorous enthusiasts and equally vocal denunciators. Certainly improvisation is not the rough and ready solution acting as a stop gap which we call 'making do'. In simple terms, improvisation may be thought of as expression in terms of invention, exploration and experimentation. In all three cases there is free unfettered approach which is restlessly inquisitive, never content with the first solution, but constantly devising deeper and more searching possibilities. Taking a simple exercise of sitting down, having dispensed with all the conventional responses, the improviser may experiment with changes of speed, sitting lightly or heavily. He may find other ways of sitting on the chair using its arms, its back, its side. He may lounge or squat, sit bolt upright, lie, curl, lean on the chair. The chair itself may become a throne, a bicycle saddle, a horse, a motor-car seat. The actor goes on to explore all the possibilities working from his initial conventional responses towards highly imaginative and fantastic extensions. The need is for lively responsiveness, not as a result of carefully thought out plans, but from exploration spontaneously, imaginatively and freely developed. This spontaneity is vital to drama. The ability to create shows spontaneous imagination at work. Many simple objects allow this kind of experimentation, such as sticks, poles, hoops, boxes with lids, strings or beads, lengths of rubber tubing, feather boas. The improvisation can be developed into a dramatic sequence where character and situation are precisely indicated with action and speech.

Improvisation of a somewhat different kind can take place in relationship to the text of a play. Here the object is to acquire a deeper understanding of the play, its plot, characters and mood. For a while strict adherence to the text is abandoned and the actors experiment. They find out how the words might be said in a different style or vocabulary. They might investigate how they personally would behave in the circumstance, they might explore aspects of the characters not noted in the text. They dig down below the surface of the text to ferret out feelings, ideas and responses to enrich what is finally selected as the truthful rather than conventional reading of the text. In some cases the improvisation begins before any study of the text to allow the actors to get to know each other and work together without the constraints of the play texts. This technique has aroused considerable controversy. It raises problems for the author, director and actor.

There is a rehearsal technique, childishly simple, worth anybody's consideration. A group of actors sit in a circle. One begins a story, trying to speak directly from his subconscious, offering images which float in his mind. As soon as he hesitates, lost for a word, the next actor picks up the story instantly, indulging HIS imagination, sharing HIS vision. There is no effort to please, no attempt to force the images, no sophisticated ratiocination. The story may last for hours. It is often excitingly rude. What is achieved in this free form verbal jazz is a sort of group consciousness, no less valuable for being childish, no less honest for being artificially engendered.*

Whether what is involved is spontaneous improvisation or that related to the play text, certain factors remain constant. Improvisation depends first upon direct, individual experience, physical, sensory and intellectual and secondly, on projected experience gained through reading, seeing films, television and talk. Many experiences in life have to be obtained at second hand, but this does not necessarily discount their validity, so long as the different nature of the experience is allowed. The richer his experiences, the more on which the participant has to draw. He must, however, have the ability which we may call imagination, to apply that experience within the context of the improvisation. He has to re-order his previous experience and relate it to the present task synthesising these memories, feelings and responses into a cohesive whole. It is important that the earlier experiences are not simply copied and reproduced. The essential truth that they contain must be extracted and re-created in terms of the present moment. This imaginative process will vary tremendously between individuals and in some develop very slowly. Speed however is not of the first importance. Time must be allowed for the process to develop without undue haste and pressure.

Improvisation also depends on observation. Detailed and careful attention

* David Benedictus in *Flourish*, vol. 2, no. 6 (Spring 1971).

must be paid to human characteristics, the manner in which people walk, the means by which feelings are revealed, the handling and manipulation of objects such as tools, machinery, the moods contained in a particular situation. The excitement of the football crowd for example combines two opposites, the elation of the winning supporters and the despondency of the losers.

A certain amount of physical skill is important in improvisation. The more freely, flexibly and unself-consciously the person can move, the greater the range of physical responses thus available to him. The more things one can do, the greater the potential vocabulary of expression becomes. The word 'potential' is important. Mere physical acrobatics are seldom required. The physical action is not an end in itself but a *means* of expression. The action itself may be the expression – there is indeed a language of movement – but in improvisation, the action is absorbed into the dramatic intention. Any facility gained in movement can feed directly into the improviser's vocabulary of physical expression.

There is a great diversity in the meaning of the word 'improvisation'. It may involve invention, exploration, elucidation, observation. All these activities lead to a spontaneous and imaginative response in words and actions that can be free and open ended or shaped into a dramatic structure. With all these alternatives, it is worth while knowing which of them you are engaged in at any one time.

Confusion sometimes arises in improvisation work because of a lack of clarity in identity. In introductory activities with a class it is usually best to begin by experimenting with, and developing responses from, their own personal experience. However, in drama, one is seldom expected to be oneself. Much more frequently an essentially different character has to be created. Personal responses, experiences and skills must be projected into a pattern that creates another person. Obviously the task becomes more complex. What could be valid in terms of one's own response does not automatically apply to the character being created. The search has to be deeper, the questioning more stringent so that the projected character has a depth and personality capable of being sustained through the situations of the improvised scenes or the script of a play. This duality of identity is inherent in any characterisation. The performer remains uniquely himself yet utilises all his imagination and skill to project another 'persona'. In developing work from personal improvisation, superficial mimicry and stereotype must be avoided. Improvisation is not playing charades. Perhaps a few extremely simple examples will serve to draw together some of the points that have been made. Pupils in a group are each invited to sit on a chair and to notice precisely what their position is. They then change to another position and fix the details clearly in mind. They then revert to the initial position and try to invent a motive for changing from the first to the second position. Although the instruction sounds mechanical it does identify the issue of motive. Alternatively the group members adopt sitting positions that express a particular (self-chosen) feeling or mood and then try to sustain the mood in other actions, standing, walking about, etc.

It is tempting for the teacher to make too precise suggestions concerning the character, the situation, the mood. Ideally these responses should stem from the performer. The suggestions simply provide a pattern or sequence. Every individual in that group should develop a personal response so that a diverse and varied series of improvisations are set in action. So often the teacher's imagination is racing, whilst the pupils' remain unstirred. The teacher's ideas should be stimulating rather than precisely descriptive. For example: the pupils sit embodying a sense of pride; carefully observing what attitudes they adopt, their body shape and the points of tension, they then sustain the characteristics in movement and project them into a particular characterisation of their own invention. The character is expanded physically in terms of costume, shoes, headgear and mentally by identifying feelings and attitudes. Costumes may be quickly devised from improvisation materials, or left to the imagination.

The group then work at a contrasting characteristic, e.g. servility, following through the process of exploration, projection, characterisation. Pairs of opposing characters might be combined and these create a group study from the initial ideas, dialogue being freely improvised. The starting stimulus may be an object, a situation that has something inherently dramatic about it – a closed box, a sealed envelope, an attractive jewel, a strange machine. It may be realistic, fantastic, exotic even ridiculous. In the sealed envelope, for example, consideration must be given to the method or arrival, the opening and the revelation of contents. If a group of people is involved, there is a choice of recipient, the response to information withheld or revealed. (A scene very close to this situation occurs almost at the end of Arnold Wesker's *Roots*. The group having experimented with their own reaction could move to an improvisation of that particular scene.)

A vital factor is, of course, the age and interests of the class. The teacher will need to observe and take note of ideas and possibilities that arise in the classroom situation and in casual conversation with children and observations in the playground. His knowledge and interest in the work they do at school and elsewhere, their hobbies and interests will also help. All these points of contact can supply material for improvisation.

In the realm of fantasy, many exciting possibilities exist. One junior class during a craft lesson constructed a golden tree. Beginning with a tree branch sprayed gold, fantastic shaped leaves formed from hessian stiffened with size were wired on. Large fruits (made from plastic play-balls) were added. They contained seeds which when chewed were alleged to make the taster invisible. This property was used by several groups each of which devised different stories surrounding this central theme. All the characters and the events were their own creation.

At a more realistic level, bells, buzzers, secret formulae might prove useful starting points. A buzzer has an imperious, demanding note. It offers a host of improvisations, such as a call for interview, a warning sign, a secret code, a dentist's surgery. Responses will, of course, vary between the operator and the summoned. In all cases the basic formula is similar: a stimulus sufficiently exciting to provoke a response that can be explored or expanded in dramatic terms. It is important that improvisations are not extended over too great a length of time. One should be content with reasonably brief episodes. As experience is enlarged, the length can be extended.

Sometimes characters can be developed from verbal portraits. Mayhew's *London Characters* contains some vivid descriptions of Cockney characters. The Watercress Girl, or the Street Conjurer, for example, contain a wealth of detail not only of physical appearance, but work and life style.

Before discussing the matter of improvisation with text, it is worth observing that whilst improvisation can be a completely satisfying activity on its own, it can also be a valuable introduction to a number of other activities. Its relationship to role play is discussed in Chapter 8, but it may also be helpful in lessons concerned with Civics, Court procedures, Councils and Parliament as well as interviews for jobs, university places or career guidance.

Improvisation with text
David Holbrook in *Thieves and Angels* has adapted a small section from Shakespeare's *Henry IV* to make a play called *Falstaff at Gadshill*. It concerns the duping of Falstaff by the Prince and Poins. In simplified terms the significant dramatic features are:

> Characters: *Prince* lively, athletic, good swordsman, intelligent, enjoys leg-pulling.
> *Falstaff* fat, boasting, fond of food and drink.
> *Poins* cheeky, astute. A joker, confidant of the Prince.
> *Gadshill, Peto, Bardolph* country bumpkins, unheroic.

These characters can be explored and tricks, boasting and fights improvised – fights that involve success, defeat and avoidance.

The plot conveniently divides into three sections:

(1) Planning the robbery. Disguises. Second plan to play joke on Falstaff.

(2) Gadshill. Hiding the horse. The two battles.
(3) Boasting at the Inn. Falstaff's discomforture.

Each of these sequences allow a good deal of invention and improvisation and finally perhaps, an appreciation of Shakespeare's solution.

Some teachers find this approach to improvisation very rewarding since the end had a more defined quality and if chosen correctly gives a dramatic shapeliness to the conclusion. It is not, of course, always necessary to refer to the source material initially. The way into a play may well be through improvisation related to a character, situation conflict or dilemma close to a pupil's own experience. Many plays that on the surface may appear difficult become amenable through an improvisation approach. The nagging yet over-protective mother and ne'er-do-well son relationship leads to such diverse plays as *Peer Gynt* and *Billy Liar*. The foster-mother/child relationship can prepare for *The Caucasian Chalk Circle*. The reverse process is also possible. The 'distanced' objective character of the play can lead to a discussion of nearer, more immediate personal responses. The more difficult the play, the more necessary to discover relationships that will help to make its meaning and intentions clearer. Many Shakespeare scenes benefit from this treatment and allows the pupil to recognise the human reality of a situation even though it is cloaked in apparently artificial language and set in an obscure period.

Perhaps the greatest danger in improvisation is superficiality, incoherence in development and vagueness in shape. Skilled actors recognise these dangers and do not allow them to become restrictive, but with the inexperienced a sense of direction and purpose must be established.

Nothing has been said so far to exclude the use of language in improvisation and to make a separation would be artificial. It is, however, convenient to look at improvisation and language separately simply to identify those characteristics which are different from the physical elements. Some suggestions concerning the development of vocal skills are contained in the section *Relationship with English*. Here we are primarily concerned with language and action. At a primitive, basic level almost unconscious vocalisation will occur whenever any vigorous activity takes place. Wrestlers are nicknamed the 'grunt and groaners'. These grunts, groans and puffs are dynamically related to the action. Impromptu language, usually a single word or short phrase, will occur at moments of stress, surprise, irritation or fear. Again the sound responses are an integral part of the one experience. This should be the aim throughout, to make the language to be appropriate to the action. Perhaps Hamlet's advice to the Players is apposite here.

Suit the action to the word, the word to the action, with this special observance, that you o'erstep not the modesty of nature: for anything so o'erdone is from the purpose of playing, whose end both at the first, and now, was and is, to hold as 'twere the mirror up to nature, to show virtue her own feature, scorn her own image, and the very age and body of the time his form and pressure.

(III. ii. 17–25)

Whilst we might be a little surprised at Hamlet's presumption in giving advice to professional actors, yet the general tenor of the speech is the right one, the matching of action and language so that one complements the other to create an effect of naturalness in observation and feeling. Hamlet goes on to complain of theatricality which unbalances the relationship by excessive gesture, coarse ranting and intrusive, inconsequential jesting that detracts from the serious progress of the action.

The partnership of word and action may become strained because of the uneven development of the two aspects. Some pupils achieve an extraordinary facility in language but remain very limited physically. Conversely, others though fluent physically may become, because of self consciousness, shyness or hesitancy remarkably limited vocally. All kinds of factors contribute to this limitation: lack of vocabulary, home situation, reading and listening habits, social pressures, accepted modes and registers of language. Progress will be slow and any improvement will show only after a long period of effort. At every stage encouragement is needed. The improvisation session can supply an opportunity for experiment, not afforded in other situations, where the pupil, inescapably himself, can extend and enrich his experience.

A considerable body of literature is devoted to movement, dance and improvisation. Numbers of the books describe particular approaches with individual variations. Background information concerning the system is necessary. Besides the Laban analysis noted in the foregoing chapter, there is Margaret Morris's approach described in *My Life in Movement*, the Joos/Leader method in Jane Winearls' *Modern Dance*, Vera Gray and Rachel Percival's approach with very strong music links, described in *Music, Movement and Mime for Children*. A rewarding book is Diana Jordan's *Childhood and Movement* which puts the whole subject in an educational perspective and would be a suitable introduction to Rudolph Laban's approach outlined in *Modern Educational Dance* and thoroughly explored in Lisa Ullman's edition of his *Mastery of Movement*. The wider implications are also discussed in V. Bruce's *Dance and Dance Drama in Education*. Books such as Peter Lofthouse's *Dance*, Janet Goodrich's *Drama in the Primary School*, Betty Lowndes's *Movement and Drama in the Primary School* show movement ideas being extended in terms of drama. Specific groups and categories of movement and dance are discussed in Joan Russell's *Creative Dance in Primary School* and *Creative Dance in the*

Secondary School, Jean Carroll and Lofthouse's *Dance for Boys,* and Bruce and Tooke's *Lord of the Dance.* (Further suggestions are listed in the Bibliography). Each of the systems listed above has its devotees and critics and no comparative evaluation is being offered. It is important that the teacher is able to identify the fundamental principles of any system so that his teaching does not simply consist of lifting ideas from a variety of texts and failing to embark on any individual exploration because of an inability to understand the basic principles.

Perhaps any reading on improvisation should begin with a look at Stanislavski's writings. Sonia Moore's *The Stanislavski System* is a good introduction. His own book *Building a Character* makes fascinating reading. Charles McGraw in *Acting is Believing* utilises the Stanislavski system in a series of practical exercises. So far as improvisation is concerned Hodgson and Richards' *Improvisation* is an important milestone. Part 1 of that book with thoughtful discussion on improvisation, its nature and purpose, identifies issues, fundamentally important to the understanding of the teacher. Creative dramatics is not a phrase that is readily connected with improvisation in England, but Geraldine Siks's *Creative Dramatics for Children,* Nellie McCaslin's *Creative Dramatics in the Classroom* with Viola Spolin's *Improvisation for the Theatre* represent important transatlantic contributions to the notion of improvisation in educational drama. A number of teacher's handbooks such as Peter Chilver's *Improvised Drama,* Kenneth Pickering's *Drama Improvised* and Donald Lightwood's *Creative Drama* offer useful and practical suggestions for the inexperienced teacher.

Improvisation is essentially a participatory activity. Teachers will benefit by attending any courses that allow personal experience at an adult level. Improvisation is basically a serious and thoughtful activity despite the apparently crazy or fantastic manifestations that arise. The teacher needs to keep his own skill and sensitivity sharp.

3

Drama and English

LANGUAGE

A traditional relationship arising from their common concern with the art and skill of language and literature has long existed between English and drama. Bertram Joseph's scholarly study *Elizabethan Acting* informs us that the education of the Elizabethan schoolboy included a study of oratory, an activity very close to acting with its instructions concerning precise vocalisation, stance and gesture. Long before this, the Athenian schoolboy was trained to speak poetry and to dance in order to perform in dramatic festivals. Unfortunately, the relationship between the two subjects has not always been a happy one. The speech element in English has sometimes received rather formal elocutory attention and, until very recently, in terature examinations, dramatic texts were treated in the same way as any other forms of literature with academic questions that ignored any suggestion of performance. One must, of course, have sympathy with the sensitive English teacher who hears a great play mangled on the stage, but it is inescapable that apart from certain closet dramas, plays are written for performance. The text of a play is essentially and substantially different from that of a novel. The latter represents the author's final, polished statement offered directly to the reader. The text of a play is a scenario that invites presentation through the medium of actors. The script is simply a beginning. It will be subjected to intense scrutiny and analysis. The performers will endeavour to interpret the meaning as they see it and the process of interpretation gives rise to a whole range of possibilities. It is comparatively easy over the course of a few years to see strikingly contrasted interpretations of a Shakespeare play. Certainly argument over the precise nature of Hamlet's character has roused more controversy than the study of any equivalent fictional hero of novel or poem. In the matter of language, the whole problem of delivering a text with due regard for its literary form and style poses many difficulties. Further complications have arisen more recently in the reaction against the formal organisation of words and language by the playwright; actors are invited to invent or 'improvise' the dialogue. Some plays demand a specific audience response before they can proceed. Samuel Beckett has written a play without words.

At least three aspects must be considered: (i) the genesis of spoken language, (ii) the development of written language particularly literature, and (iii) the language element in drama.

Lloyd James in *Our Spoken Language* vividly describes the origins of speech:

> The raw material out of which speech is made consists of the noises that Man, provided his is normal, is able to make by adapting his breathing, smelling, and tasting apparatus to the production of noises. ... He uses a lot of extraneous energy as well, making facial gestures, and flinging his arms about gesticulating, and frequently using many of his muscles in one way or another. ... He handles his breathing apparatus in such a way that his breath stream creates in the surrounding air pulsations, variations of pressure of different kinds, explosions, frictions, hisses, buzzes, puffs, hums, musical and unmusical noises all charged with a wonderful significance to him and to those in earshot who 'understand' him. ... The spoken language is ... perceived by the ear. The printed or written language is made by the hand and perceived by the eye. ... The fact is that the two forms of language, aural and visual have nothing in common except the bond of understanding.

We are made aware of the gulf separating spoken and written language. Speech at its best is rather like an erupting volcano in which the flowing lava burns, glows and spits with vivid and intense activity driven by an explosive internal force. In print that speech may resemble the same lava, cooled, grey, immobile, dusty. The written form of language is a result of a complex process beginning with the translation of thought into words, and the ordering of those words into patterns that conform to or sometimes deliberately reject established conventions of writing developed over the centuries. The writer continually polishes and revises as he searches for the more precise, evocative, poetic, or beautiful. Finally there comes the committal to print and the author hopes that the reader will respond to those formalised black marks on the page with an intensity that reflects the force of the original impetus. The playwright has to go through a further creative process. He is anxious for the 'volcanic' quality to be sustained. He is obliged to use written language for the dialogue and he has to devise a third type of language – 'written/spoken'. The style may be flowing, poetic, orderly with particular attention paid to aural and rhythmic qualities or apparently haphazard and everyday. But there is always an intensely sensitive selection and organisation of words and phrases having regard for their meaning, sound, rhythm and metaphoric qualities. The task of interpreting and recreating the speech from the text is entrusted to the actor. It is obviously complicated and demanding.

Fluency and imaginative vitality are important requisites as well as some expertise in the technical aspects of voice and speech. Also required is some understanding of different literary and dramatic forms and their interpretation.

The study of English and the study of drama in school in order to be mutually profitable must each have this concern for spoken language. Indeed the study of linguistics urges us to think and respond afresh in this matter. Both will be concerned with the understanding and appreciation of literature, particularly dramatic literature, and in the creative aspects of play-making, writing and production. This is obviously a long-term and complex process. At various stages in a pupil's career at school emphasis will be differently placed, but it must be recognised that activities in both disciplines can be mutually beneficial if their true relationship is recognised.

STORY TELLING

Story telling is one of the oldest and most famous arts and the teacher should strive to develop some personal skill in the art. The story teller creates a very special living relationship with his listeners, drawing upon an ancient oral tradition, acquainting them with new words, phrases, expressions, showing a sustained narrative line, illustrating the compelling attractiveness of good vocalisation and extending the imaginative experience of the listeners. At least, all this is possible in telling a story in the classroom. Every dull, cliché-ridden, unimaginative story is a lost opportunity. Conversation can arise naturally from a story, but it is unwise to follow every tale with questions. Another kind of response might be more suitable. So often a story which the author has struggled to formulate with painstaking care is destroyed by a crude reduction to black and white question and answer. The teacher should try to estimate what is particularly attractive – the quality of the language, the rhythm, new words, the novel situation, possibilities for drama, a stimulus for painting or craft work – and concentrate on just one or two aspects. It should never be forgotten, however, that a story or a poem is a creation in its own right. Questions and follow-ups may be superfluous. Sometimes the story can simply be told and that is all. With good examples before them, the children should be encouraged to develop their story-telling skills. Often there is a natural raconteur in the class, but his talents should not be over-used.

Story, like drama, in its simplest form is a combination of character and plot narrated in a way that absorbs and interests the audience. When a story is being prepared by the teacher or the class it should be recognised that it is not always appropriate to build in chronological sequence. The description of vivid characters of contrasting qualities who confront each other at a particularly exciting moment which ends up as the climax of the story may well be a good starting point. Later the preceding events and a conclusion may be added so that finally the story flows smoothly from start to finish. Children and teacher can combine in this process by contributing character studies, suggesting incidents or plots, beginnings and endings. A narrative might well develop from a visual stimulus.

Here is an extremely simple example taken with a class of junior children. They were shown and allowed to handle a miniature imitation snake that one of them had brought into class. It curled and twisted as it was handled. The children were invited to invent a name for the snake. Everyone's suggestion was heard and each jotted down his idea. Some names were ordinary and familiar such as Harold, Bill and Jack, whilst others sought for onomatopoeic effects with Sammy, Slimy, Slinky. Others suggested jungle locations – Sabu, Umgala. The more exciting names were those that did something in excess of providing a mere label. They sought to suggest particular vocal effects or allusive connections. The class were then asked to describe the movement of the snake. Such words as slithered, slid, crawled, coiled, emerged. Verbalising the idea was the prime intention. Next a location was invented for the coiled snake and gradually a lively little story emerged as the creature's activities and adventures were imagined. The object itself caused no feelings of fear and was sufficiently exciting to invite a quick imaginative response and to inspire the development of a spoken story. If we analyse this example, the requirements become obvious – a stimulating idea to initiate response (i.e. something to talk about) a search for words that will both accurately describe and enhance particularly by their aural and figurative qualities and the need to shape the material into a meaningful and dramatic pattern for narration.

Vocabulary is acquired by all kinds of verbal experience, story telling, everyday conversations, exercises in expressing sensory responses, even collecting word lists. The words need to be absorbed into the child's personal vocabulary and this can be achieved only through constant use and practice. The skill required is twofold. First, is ability to respond in conversation and secondly, to sustain a rather longer explanation, description or narration. Conversation lessons can become very dull and stereotyped if the teacher makes no preparation. There must always be a stimulus of some kind. It may come from a child telling of a family celebration or of an incident on the way home. It may be a response to an event in school. As well as these, the teacher should always have an extensive supporting store of materials, objects, poems, jingles, stories capable of evoking strong and lively responses. It is important that this early language work is not too demanding. One must be content with the apt and brief rather than strain after extended and artificial effects. This training in oral effectiveness ought to take place in casual conversation as well as in the more structured situation. Telling jokes, asking riddles, relating brief anecdotes should precede any attempts at longer narratives. Much of this informal work may acquire a distinctly dramatic quality by the use of distinctive voices for the characters in a story. This the teacher should encourage.

Moving from speaking aloud to reading aloud we need to remind ourselves of the differences between these two activities. Story telling is also distinct from story writing in that each demands its own particular and special skills. Speaking is putting into words inner ideas that demand outward expression. The attributes of spoken language are utilised. Reading aloud consists of recognising a series of signals in print that must be translated into speech. There are occasional hints concerning expression such as exclamation marks, full stops, quotation marks or underlinings suggesting the spoken pattern or emphasis, but generally the reader is required to devise a pattern for himself from what he observes on the page. This will depend largely upon his previous experience. The child will need frequent opportunities to explore and experiment with these very different tasks. In reading, the words are provided and the overall shape suggested. In speech, both word and pattern have to be invented. There is a further skill in the construction of a narrative pattern from assembled ideas.

A most informative book by Paul Gallico called *Confessions of a Story Teller* is illuminating on this process of story making. Teachers would be well advised to read it. Side by side with the completed short stories are the scraps of information, newspaper reports, and other details of the events from which the stories were developed. Story writing is a completely different activity from oral narration. Any experienced teacher of young juniors will tell you of the gap between spoken and written skills and how frequently they have been disappointed by the written work of apparently fluent and imaginative speakers. Written work, however simple, is related to the pattern of literary forms having a style and composition quite different from the spoken tradition.

PLAY-MAKING AND SCRIPT WRITING

The construction of a play script is an extremely complex process. The teacher introducing this work with his pupils should proceed warily. With younger children play-making will arise from improvisation. Occasionally quite young children express a desire to write a play and the opportunity afforded by this request should not be lost. Generally speaking though, the drama should not be contained within the rigidity of the set text with words laboriously learned. Only as the children grow in experience and sophistication should the intricacies of script making be introduced. The transmutation of speech into written text is an attempt to change one style or mode of language into another, and each style adheres to substantially different rules. Furthermore in play scripts, the dialogue has to perform the multiple function of establishing situation, character and mood, as well as carrying the burden of the plot.

Experiments in writing dialogue might be started by simple question and answer situations such as quizzes which require the compiler to grapple with words and form them into coherent questions. It is quite useful to list words that demonstrate the range and variety of language. A collection of jokes and riddles written down and then read aloud will introduce ideas of humour, timing, climax, dramatic pause. The more understanding of the function of dramatic dialogue that can be absorbed by the pupil, the more likely will be his own attempts to be successful.

Dialogue can initiate action. Putting instructions or requests into words is a useful beginning. It will be seen however that an apparently simple request invites much more careful attention. The speaker and the listener need to be characterised. The invitation or order implies a certain situation and mood which might be pleasant or unpleasant. It is important from the start that the character's speeches should be written in a style appropriate to him. Brief character sketches placed alongside the dialogue help to guide and amplify. Initially this process is bound to be crude, but persistence will develop thoughtfulness and subtlety. Writing dialogue that creates a particular mood and feeling is difficult to achieve, but some exploration of the means by which attitudes indicative of mood are conveyed should be attempted.

The whole intention of this introductory work is to encourage a recognition of the multiple functions of language as it is used in dialogue and script writing.

Some useful experience can be gained by devising scripts from literature in which the bones of a dialogue already exist. Using the information about the characters and the situation already available, the dialogue can be expanded and the episode translated into a dramatic form. The Mad Hatter's Tea Party from *Alice's Adventures in Wonderland* provides a convenient illustration. The characters are very clearly delineated: the March Hare, The Hatter, the Dormouse and Alice. The scene at Alice's entry is well described and the conversation easily adapted to the dialogue of a play script. There is opportunity to deal with instructions such as 'in an encouraging way', 'looking with great curiosity'. The pupils might include some riddles of their own when the conversation reaches that point and they could invent a conclusion of their own. The list of rules that Gulliver has to agree to in order to gain release from his bondage in Lilliput implies a great deal of debate in the King's court. Various Ministers are clearly concerned about provisions for travel, war and food. The framing of the conditions and their submission to Gulliver could provide an entertaining dramatic sequence. The ballad of *John Gilpin* contains some very suitable dialogue. Several incidents in that poem lend themselves to play-making and script writing. For older pupils, the first conversation on the bus between Vic and Ingrid in Stan Barstow's *A Kind of Loving* provides a start for the dialogue but it also invites conjecture as to methods by which the thoughts that the novelist interposes between the speeches can be translated into words to suggest attitudes and feelings. Wole Soyinka's poem 'Telephone Conversation' is a very dramatic dialogue in which only one speaker is heard. Some teachers might feel that the poem would be spoilt by giving it dramatic treatment. In this case it could be used as an example from which to devise another situation involving the telephone and an urgent inquiry.

With the acquisition of some skill in writing dialogue, recognising the particular requirements of drama, pupils might attempt brief sketches, episodes or short plays of their own. Questions will arise about the initiation of a play idea, the search for material, the ordering of the various elements. Examination of play scripts and discussion of their techniques can be valuable at this point. Often this provides a fresh approach to a play text and for some children the means of interesting them when other approaches have failed. The question of style and form will crop up. By looking at examples such as the Witches' scene in *Macbeth* on the one hand, to brief radio sketches such as Harold Pinter's *Black and White* on the other, a vast range of styles and techniques can be observed. The pupils' first efforts will be marred in form, but anyone showing particular aptitudes should be encouraged and their work looked at with care and sympathy. Negative criticism of faults should be avoided.

Non-dramatic literature contains a vast store of stories and poems that allow effective dramatic treatment if certain criteria are observed. The original author presumably selected the narrative or poetic form rather than dramatic because he felt it best fitted what he desired to express. The teacher needs to exercise some care in his selection of non-dramatic literature for dramatisation otherwise he might tackle, or suggest that his children tackle unrewarding pieces. It is possible to identify the characteristics of narrative prose or poetry suitable for dramatic use. Important features include: a strong sense of conflict, easily identifiable characters, ideas that stimulate active investigation and physical movement; a linear development with shape and climax. Unless at least some of these factors are present it is unlikely that drama will readily develop. The narrative may simply provide ideas for improvisation. Any snippet of dialogue in the narrative could provide the basis of a script. Exciting incidents may be dramatised through spoken or acted scripts. The activity must give attention to (i) the identification of location by use of sound effects or introductory dialogue, e.g. Lorenzo's 'How sweet the moonlight sleeps upon this bank! Here will we sit', etc.; (ii) the identification of characters and a means of introducing them; (iii) a sequence of events that will contribute to the dramatic effects of suspense and climax; (iv) the style of the dialogue; (v) additional effects such as music, background noises, weather which contributes to the general mood of the play. The Russian playwright Chekhov is a master of subtle sound effects. Noises of tapping sticks, wind, rain, breaking wires and snatches of song contribute vitally to the mood conveyed by the stage action. The need for adaptation and re-ordering will arise and this should be allowed as a perfectly acceptable practice. Shakespeare certainly never hesitated in rewriting history to suit his particular dramatic purpose.

The poem *John Gilpin* mentioned earlier can be the basis of an excellent little play, even though at first glance it would seem wildly unsatisfactory with its rapidly changing scenes, carriages and runaway horses. Three locations, Gilpin's shop, the balcony of the Inn and the Callender's house can easily accommodate the story. The discussion of the outing and the commencement, with John being delayed by customers, and the final breathless departure with the clanging wine bottles can all take place in the shop. The family and in-laws crowded on to the balcony have a good opportunity of creating the excitement of John's ride and pursuit by the post-boy (cf. the race in Synge's *Playboy of the Western World*). A brief episode at the Callender's is followed by the final reunion at the Inn. The patches of dialogue in the poem identify certain characteristics of Mr and Mrs Gilpin and the flighty servant girl. The play may suggest versifying treatment. Hints on costumes and properties abound and the whole poem can be realised in quite an exciting way. This is only an example, but it does contain the characteristics required. Greek myths, medieval folk tales, stories of exploration, adventure, space exploits – the resources are endless but selectivity is vital. Stories with extended descriptions, excessively complex plots, rapidly changing locations or swarms of characters are not appropriate. It is far better to choose a single episode from a longer story rather than attempt to encapsulate the whole narrative in a miniature drama. A fine play was made by a group of senior boys from episodes in the novel *Escape from Colditz*. Plans of the escape route were drawn up and then translated to the classroom space. Characters were selected and dossiers of their particular personalities were compiled. Episodes in the prison and at the railway station made good exciting dramatic material.

SPEECH AND LANGUAGE IN DRAMA

It will have become apparent that speech and language in drama have many distinctive qualities which make extensive technical and aesthetic demands. In summarising the characteristics of dramatic language we find

(i) the form is almost always dialogue, although it will include long soliloquies as well as thinly disguised narrative or descriptive sections; (ii) it has to supply the bulk of information concerning the plot and the characters; (iii) it has to carry the literary weight of the play; and (iv) it attempts to evoke the special and individual atmosphere of the play. The last two elements are achieved chiefly through literary style which can vary from the apparently, haphazard, inconsequential conversation between the rugger players in David Storey's *The Changing Room* to the formal, poetic challenges which identify the conflict at the opening of *Richard II*. In both cases the words accompanying the action must appear to be both spontaneous and appropriate. Obviously for these requirements to be effectively carried out, considerable expertise is necessary; technically in the vocalisation, interpretively in relation to the characters and events and stylistically as dictated by the particular literary mode in which the author has elected to write. At professional performances we take these skills for granted and are disappointed when they are absent. It would be unusual, however, for the drama work in school to be directed towards producing recruits for the acting profession, so the teacher must estimate what his precise expectations are so far as language in drama is concerned and how they might be brought to fruition.

Formal speech training and elocution have fallen into disrepute, sometimes for good reasons but also for others less defensible. Perfection of articulation and tone tended to detract from the necessary vitality and naturalness. Material for speaking inclined to be poetic, high-styled, romantic and sentimental, far removed from everyday and, indeed, stage usage. The pupil appeared to be acquiring vocal tricks rather than general skills. A great deal of work by progressive teachers has, in recent years, removed most of these criticisms and much imaginative and lively speech work is being done. The basic requirements for good speech remain unaltered. Effective breath control, clear articulation, projection, variety of pitch and tone are still necessary, though the methods by which they are acquired have changed. As an instrument of expression, the voice had many demands made on it. It is required to operate in many different situations and in each case the need is different. Broadly speaking, pupils must be encouraged to use their voices effectively and avoid lapsing into choked silence when questions are addressed to them or in conversation. Confidence in speaking is vitally important. So far as the listener is concerned it is necessary for him to actually hear what the speaker has said. This requires a skill in audibility and projection. There should be a meaningful connection between the speaker and what he is saying. Hence the need for sensitivity and flexibility.

If these basic requirements are satisfied, then pupils are on the way to achieving reasonable speech skills and their work in drama is likely to be more successful. The teacher will need to have some knowledge of the technical aspects that will aid development and be ready to offer advice when the need arises to overcome a difficulty whether it is to do with breathing, articulation, projection or pronunciation. The presence of a dominating regional accent or dialect may seem to create an extra problem, but the requirements listed above apply *whatever* accent is being employed. The aim should be to encourage flexibility in vocalisation together with an ability to respond in the appropriate register of speech. It is impossible to prescribe a particular method of speech training. Some teachers prefer the occasional corrective comment, while others follow a more formal pattern of speech education. It is important that the teacher is well informed and that his personal training and skill is sufficient to equip him to meet the needs when they arise. He should have some knowledge of breath control, the articulation of English vowels and consonants, tone and projection and an understanding of the nature of speech tune, stress and pitch. The worst possible method is the simple invitation to imitate the style of the teacher. Any kind of game or informal activity that draws attention to sounds, quizzes, spelling bees, speech games, tongue twisters, synonyms and antonyms, foreign equivalents, will help to establish ear training and vocal responsiveness.

As well as the technical aspects, meaning, expression, style and interpretation are important and vitally so in drama. Meaningfulness is of prime importance. This implies understanding and comprehension. The most beautiful enunciation that is devoid of meaning is but a hollow echo. In a poem or novel the author can fill out his meaning with extended passages of description or explanation, but in drama the meaning is so often contained in an implication, an irony, a play on words depending on the character and the scene to acquire its complete significance. Having discerned an acceptable meaning, the words still have to be translated into vocal utterance. The sounds that issue forth must project the intended meaning. This is not easily done. A misplaced stress, a changed inflection can alter the meaning. Neither is it possible for the words to have an objective reality. They are inevitably interpreted by the speaker. His concept of the character, his views of the situation may well distort the author's original intention and produce an inaccurate or incongruous interpretation. Perhaps it is easiest to think of meaning as being the author's intention and of interpretation of the translation of that meaning into speech and action. It is preferable for attention to be given to the former before attempting the latter.

The playwright also chooses to write in a particular style, using poetry or prose. The language adopted may be high flown and exotic or the unembellished ordinary. The style selected is that which the writer considers to be the most effective linguistic vehicle for his purpose. This choice is deliberate. It is therefore necessary to become familiar with different literary modes and styles since they are obviously important when speaking the script. Timing is also important. Dialogue depends upon the ebb and flow of sound, the dramatic pause, the quick retort, the slow measured explanation or the quiet recollection. The speakers have to learn to respond and co-operate with sensitivity. Two examples might serve to illustrate the complex relationship of style, timing and sensitivity.

Harold Pinter's *The Birthday Party* opens with an exchange between Petey, a deckchair attendant, and his wife Meg, who runs a boarding house in a somewhat seedy seaside resort. He has been out to work early and has returned for breakfast. The conversation consists of a series of almost monosyllabic exchanges which are repetitive and dull. 'Is that you?' is repeated three times. Referring to the cornflakes offered to Petey for his breakfast, Meg chirps 'Are they nice? I thought they'd be nice.' These gems are interspersed with short and longer pauses as Meg appears and disappears behind the kitchen serving hatch. Clearly the reiteration of the phrases, the pauses, the paucity of vocabulary are all part of Pinter's design. A good deal of skill in timing, voice tone and contrast is necessary. Perhaps Petey speaks in a monotone, whilst Meg uses a bright, lively attack. This conversation continues for several pages. The words have the appearance of total ordinariness but they really represent a tightly constructed vocal pattern. Later that characteristic repetitiveness flares into a spectacular extension of violence and fearful cross questioning.

At first glance the style and construction of Shakespeare's *King Lear* might seem to have little in common with Pinter's play, yet there is an equal concern for language and the effects it can create. In the opening scene of *Lear*, Kent attempts to dissuade the King from rejecting Cordelia by a courageous appeal couched in forceful terms!

> Be Kent unmannerly
> When Lear is mad. What woulds't thou do, old man?
> Think'st thou that duty shall have dread to speak,
> When power to flattery bows? To plainness honour's bound,
> When majesty falls to folly.
>
> (I. i. 146–148)

Careful examination of these lines reveals the dense richness of word choice and verse construction. The main antithesis contrasts majesty with folly and power bowing to flattery. The alliteration of duty, dread, falls, folly, power, plainness, the assonance of bow and bound, mannerly and mad, all combine to make a strong vocal effect and a meaningful appeal. The actor has to recognise the quality of the verse and the mode of its construction and to contain it within his concept of the character. These lines must not be rendered poetically, but as if spoken by a plain speaking nobleman to an angered King. The absorption of the style into the character is important. Bertram Joseph in *Acting Shakespeare* gives a marvellous example from *Romeo and Juliet*. He reminds us that the first exchange between Romeo and Juliet at the masked ball is written as a sonnet conforming to all the precise conventions of sonnet writing, yet at the same time managing to convey the particular intensity of the young couple's sudden and overpowering love and the individual nature of their feelings as each responds to the other's words.

It is essential for pupils when reading play scripts or acting to become sensitive to the style and qualities of language used by the playwright. Too often the reading is superficial and dull simply because of a failure to respond to the vocabulary and to recognise the figures and style in which the text is written. Perhaps the magnitude of the problem of language is not fully recognised by teachers and this may account for some of their disappointment with the oral elements in drama. It is noticeable in improvisation that the speech is usually rough, tentative and inconsequential and sometimes completely inappropriate in character. A comprehensive plan for speech education will make a vital contribution to drama and conversely drama, with its particular concern for language, and utterance, can contribute substantially to speech work.

So often reading aloud ceases after a child has learned to read, or it persists with the practice of reading round the class which is extremely limited in value. Opportunities for reading aloud must be provided, by a child presenting a piece of his own work such as an essay or poem, or perhaps a 'story time' conducted by a group of readers. Some preparation for performance should be made so that the readings have as much quality as possible. Children should be encouraged to mark their scripts when pauses, or special emphasis are required. Some punctuation for grammar does not always correspond with the needs of speech. They should become aware of the sound quality of words, contrasts and antitheses and other devices that utilise the sound or pattern of words. They should attempt to identify characters within the poem or story whose conversation is recorded by adopting a slight change of manner, tone or pitch. The teacher should ensure the children get plenty of opportunities to hear a wide range of stories, poems, drama, etc., by reading aloud himself, by using broadcasts and records all of which contribute to aural education. 'Ear training' is perhaps a rather technical description, but it is an important part of children's listening experience.

Experience in improvisation will help to develop vocal skill, but as has been noted earlier, there is a danger that the style of speech adopted, while thinly disguising the normal voice, does not really approach characterisation. Deficiencies in vocabulary, expression and limited knowledge will all be revealed in the improvisation situation. It may be that scripted drama can be of value at this point since the playwright will almost certainly have taken voice and character into account in writing his script. For example, in Wesker's *Roots* members of a family group discuss, quarrel, have parties, respond to employers, sympathise, explain political beliefs, exhort and denounce. Extracts from plays such as these can give experience of utterance in character. They may be developed freely into improvisation or lead to a closer study of the text.

In applying these techniques to drama either for play-reading or performance, it is fairly clear that the pupil will need some skill in reading aloud. He should be able to mark a script in such a way that will aid his expression and clarify the meaning and possess sufficient vocal dexterity to give at least some suggestion of character. Finally, and this comes only with plenty of experience, a response that takes account of the style of the play. It may be vigorously obvious as, for example, in the dramatised version of *Treasure Island* where Jim Hawkins's boyish tones contrast with the rough coarseness of the pirates and the more refined language of the Captain and the Squire. Subtleties of tone in character can be introduced if the reading aloud has been well tackled. Verse plays should be attempted, though one needs to be aware of rhyming couplets which so often induce a pantomimic comedy style deadly both to play and poetry. Blank verse is probably the best to begin with. Pupils should always be encouraged to put into their own words the text they are reading. This has the effect of clarifying the meaning for them and also revealing where any misunderstanding may lie. First attempts should be brief. The ability to sustain a particular style of voice, tone and expression for a period of time is acquired only with practice. Many short scripts exist which allow this kind of experience.

A wide range of play texts should be examined. The fantastic, historical, comic, scientific, serious should all be attempted. For example whilst it would be unusual for junior school children to be working with scripted plays, a fourth-year group might tackle the Mumming play *St George and the Dragon*, extracts from MacNeice's verse play *Christopher Columbus* and Ted Hughes's Nativity play *The Three Kings*. At the secondary level texts could include *Oh What a Lovely War, A Man for All Seasons, Under Milk Wood* and *The Insect Play*. Differences of dramatic treatment might be explored by comparative studies of one character as portrayed by several writers, e.g. St Joan in Shakespeare, Shaw and Anouilh. The playwrights' attitude towards characterisation as well as linguistic style may then be examined. Undoubtedly this is a very difficult area and the problem of style is not always solved satisfactorily even by professional companies.

The teaching of English and its relationship to drama is undergoing continual investigation and assessment. Frank Whitehead's *The Disappear-*

ing Dais and *New Directions in the Teaching of English*, edited by Denys Thompson, discuss some of the present trends. E. J. Burton's *Teaching English through Self-Expression* and Christopher Parry's *English through Drama* give practical suggestions on work in English and drama particularly in the area of Speech and Expression. Fowler and Dick's series *English 11/12, 12/13, 13/14, 14/15, 15/16* also contain a number of topics that relate English and drama. Musgrave Horner's *Movement, Voice and Speech*, Rose Bruford's *Speech and Drama* and Clifford Turner's *Voice and Speech in the Theatre* are texts full of advice and information on the role of speech in the theatre with considerable attention given to the technical aspects of speaking and acting.

Another group of books describe the technicalities of speech in even greater detail. They include Daniel Jones's *An Outline of English Phonetics* which classifies and describes all the sounds in English and short but helpful handbooks such as Geoffrey Crump's *A Manual of English Speech*, Greta Colson's *Speech Practice* and *Voice Production and Speech*. A number of practising teachers and lecturers have devised courses in Speech Education for children: among these are Diana Morgan's *Living Speech in the Primary School* and Arthur Wise's *Talking Together* which suggest work for junior school children. Plans for secondary schools are discussed in J. Casciani's *Speak for Yourselves*, Hodgson and Richards's *Living Expression* which includes recordings and Peter Chilver's *Talking*. Maisie Cobby is well known for her interest in play-making. *The Play-makers* and *Calling All Play-makers* suggest courses for junior and secondary schools respectively.

Accounts of individual experiences in play-making often provide interesting reading. Joan Haggerty's *Please Miss, Can I Play God?* and Paul Cornwell's *Creative Playmaking in the Primary School* are records of play-making ventures. Piaget's *Language and Thought of the Child*, David Crystall's *Linguistics* and Basil Harvey's *The Scope of Oracy* remind us of the wider implication of speech, language and communication. Teachers should make themselves familiar with at least some of their findings.

STUDY OF SCRIPTED PLAYS

Any teacher who includes the study of plays (including Shakespeare's) in his English course will need to devise a method of dealing with play scripts. It is important for the pupils to recognise the peculiar and special quality of dramatic texts that distinguish them from other forms of literature. Reference has already been made to the 'written/spoken' language that the playwright employs, but the process has other complexities. Apart from specific stage instructions ranging from the copious (e.g. G. Bernard Shaw) to the non-existent (e.g. T. S. Eliot), the playwright has to transmit most of the ideas of the plot, character, situation, mood that he wishes to establish, through the medium of dialogue. Even the most elaborate stage instructions have to be transposed into setting and action. It follows that a process of interpretation and elucidation must accompany the study if the full force of the play is to be recognised.

Whenever possible, the pupils' first confrontation with a play should be a performance, but this ideal is seldom achieved and it may be that the special complexities of certain plays need some kind of preparation. Here the teacher will have to apply his own expertise. Plays such as *Billy Liar* or *A Taste of Honey* effect an immediate impact, whilst *Hamlet* or *The Tempest* may benefit from careful preliminary exploration. It is important that the teacher does not mistake his own familiarity with the play for his students' understanding, taking for granted something that is in fact unknown to them. For a complex play or one in an unusual style, a suitable starting point for study must be clearly established. This need not necessarily be the beginning of the play, nor directly related to the text, though the teacher himself will have to be very familiar with the text, able to identify the characters with brief thumbnail sketches, and understand the main development of the action through the plot with a clear idea of the underlying theme. It is usually possible to identify a scene which is complete in itself and characteristic of the whole play or at least an important part of it. With this as a point of departure, other relevant scenes can be studied and gradually the whole structure built up. In well-written plays the individual scenes have a recognisable coherence and dramatic shape. Certain playwrights do adopt extremely eccentric styles of writing, e.g. N. F. Simpson, Ionesco, or Samuel Beckett where the normal rules clearly do not apply. In such cases an awareness of the eccentricity must be encouraged so that the pupils respond to and enjoy the style and do not expect the conventional. Simpson's *A Resounding Tinkle*, for example, depends a great deal on the comic effects associated with misplaced logic, paradox and illogical antithesis (e.g. the title). Pupils might be introduced to the play by being invited to invent their own paradoxical phrases. Much youthful humour consists of this zany, illogical approach to comedy. Martin Esslin's *The Theatre of the Absurd* is a useful Teacher's Guide to modern playwrights working in non-conventional styles.

In Arnold Wesker's *Roots*, constructed in a more orthodox way, there is a scene (the final section of II. i) in which Beatie Bryant, a young woman visiting her parents' home in a small isolated Norfolk village, talks to her mother. Mr Bryant returns home rather unexpectedly. He is feeling unwell because of a stomach complaint and he is also distressed at having just seen his pal Stan Mann taken off in an ambulance to hospital. Beatie tells her parents of the forthcoming visit by her boyfriend Ronnie, but the conversation is interrupted by the arrival of Mr Healey, a manager of the farm where Mr Bryant works as a stockman. Although Healey inquires after Bryant's health, there is an underlying threat of sacking if the ill health continues. Bryant also learns that Mann has died in the ambulance. The pain, the threat and Mann's death combine to provoke an outburst from Mr Bryant over a trivial matter of cake-baking and the pleasantry of the first exchanges contrasts vividly with the dissonant bitter family quarrel with which the scene ends.

This short episode identifies the three main characters, Mr and Mrs Bryant and Beatie and the important subsidiary character of Stan Mann. It places the main locale, the kitchen of the Bryant household, and introduces several of the major strands of the plot, the expected arrival of Ronnie, the threat to Mr Bryant's health, the intrusion of death and the underlying streak of meanness and aggression that can poison family life.

The study of such a scene might well be a starting point for examining the whole play. It is reasonably coherent in itself. It is possible to compare Mr Bryant's attitude towards his wife and daughter with the one he assumes towards Mr Healey. We get a good character sketch of Stan Mann and the family's response to his death. All these ideas could be elucidated fairly quickly and the scene easily acted. Only a few chairs are needed with a table at which Beatie is making the cake, and a parcel containing the gift Beatie has brought home for her father. Other short extracts demonstrating the relationship between Ronnie and Beatie, particularly his power over her could be explored. An example occurs in the action preceding the episode just described. Having acquired this familiarity with the main characters, the earlier scenes of the play can be dealt with without difficulty and a number of the ironies more readily recognised. The tension between the real Beatie and the 'Ronnie-dominated' Beatie will also become clear. It is vital that this conflict is recognised so that the final release is appreciated. Initially pupils will need assistance in discerning underlying themes and attitudes. Scenes that provide clear examples are helpful in the task of constructing the total pattern. It is seldom possible to act or even read a whole play in the classroom situation, but it should not be impossible to stage small important illustrative scenes.

When a play is very complex in structure and meaning, with a number of different levels of reality operating simultaneously, the elucidatory process becomes even more important. Hamlet's quarrel with Laertes epitomised in the final duel poses all kinds of questions about the play concerning characters and motivations. Discussion of the Laertes revenge theme can lead towards Hamlet's more complex dilemma with the problem of the Ghost's identity and the relationship of Claudius and Gertrude. So often in adult criticism of plays, use is made of our own previous experience of the play which is not available to the children.

Professor Christopher Ricks writing about the *Sunday Times* Shakespeare posters (*Sunday Times Magazine* no. 28, 1971) quotes Ezra Pound's view that 'the medium of drama is not words but persons moving about on a stage using words'. It is essential that pupils come to understand the triple function that words are executing by simultaneously providing dialogue, initiating action and developing characterisation. Sometimes this is very obvious, as in the case of Iago's description of the exchange of greetings between Cassio and Desdemona on her arrival in Cyprus:

> He takes her by the palm; ay, well said, whisper: with as little a web as this, will I ensnare as great a fly as Cassio. Ay, smile upon her, do; I will gyve thee in thine own courtship. You say true; 'tis so, indeed; if such tricks as these strip you out of your lieutenantry, it had been better you had not kissed your three fingers so oft, which now again you are most apt to play the sir in. Very good; well kissed! an excellent courtesy! 'tis so indeed. Yet again your fingers to your lips? would they were clyster-pipes for your sake! (Othello II. i)

Often the information is retrospective, i.e. the words describe something that has just been done. In performing such scenes a wary eye must be cast for these requirements. In the Iago speech a great deal of information is being given to the actors playing Cassio and Desdemona and their actions must precede Iago's comments or the effect is ludicrous.

The linguistic style of contemporary plays may not offer too many problems in utterance although regional accents (as in the case of *Roots*) may need some mastering. But when it comes to Shakespeare or Restoration comedy for example, then the style demands certain vocal dexterity and skill, the absence of which detracts from the reading. Recordings can be usefully employed in these cases, not necessarily of the whole play but of extracts that characterise the style. A wide range of Shakespeare recordings exist. It is even useful to compare two versions for style and interpretation. Recording companies are continually adding to their lists of play recordings and gramophone libraries are extending their stock of vocal as well as musical discs. Recordings are particularly helpful in school situations when either male or female voices are lacking. Vocal contrasts between characters which might otherwise have been lost are then established. Whilst it is best to have recordings of complete play texts, sometimes shortened versions or edited extracts (often with accompanying commentaries) can be very helpful. One is anxious to impart the feeling and coherence of the whole play, but except in very unusual circumstances, listening to a full play at one sitting would be impossible. The teacher should watch the review columns of journals for notices of play recordings. Despite the value of listening, no play study is really complete without the pupils tackling the speaking problems of the text for themselves even if the attempts are extremely brief.

Visual support is also helpful. Illustrations such as the Shakespeare posters mentioned above are valuable. Photographs of productions, newspaper cuttings and pictures especially where contrasting views or productions of the same play can be displayed all help to emphasise the unique nature of drama and the visual realisation of the text.

Teachers for whom this transmutation process is difficult will find J. L. Styan's *The Elements of Drama* a rewarding study. The chapter headings indicate the approach very clearly, e.g. 'Dramatic dialogue is more than conversation' or 'The behaviour of the words on the stage'. Professor Styan writes most illuminatingly. Whilst his book may not have an immediate relevance to the classroom, it is immensely valuable to the teacher. *Understanding Drama* by Brooks and Heilman approaches the same topic in a somewhat different way. The notes and analyses are helpful in promoting an understanding of play structures and forms.

The basic intention of play study should be to reveal the uniquely three-dimensional quality of drama – 'talking figures in space' – to which the text gives the key. Working space is obviously a major factor and in a classroom there will be severe limitations. This should not always prove an impenetrable barrier. Sometimes adjustment of the furniture is possible. Certain scenes can utilise the classroom space including the desks. Usually there is some space at the front of the classroom that will accommodate scenes between two or three people. If any scenes are to be presented as much preparation as possible should be attempted. Rehearsals should not take place with the rest of the class passively watching. This is bad for performer and audience.

The actors should be encouraged to learn their speeches and, whenever possible, simple props and costumes should be introduced. It is worth while developing a technique for this style of lesson so that the pupils will know what to expect and that properties or costumes that they provide will be used. The right atmosphere must be encouraged. The pleasure should come from the experience of something well done rather than a superficial, jokey, charade-playing atmosphere. Initially the scenes should be brief and simple, lasting perhaps five to ten minutes. Long scenes that gradually deteriorate into dull readings devoid of action should be avoided. Pupils should be encouraged to make their own prompt copies that include details of characterisation, setting, motivation, explanation of difficult words or phrases, suggestions of vocal pattern, accent and timing. Anything that will lead to a careful and thoughtful scrutiny of the text will pay dividends in understanding. When all action is out of the question rehearsed readings may be suitable substitutes, pre-recorded on tape if the equipment is available. Inventiveness with sound effects or suitable music can add another dimension to the recording. The technicalities of this activity certainly have an appeal for certain pupils and it may well be the way in which their interest in drama is aroused.

Lists of play suggestions together with more detailed information concerning techniques and procedures will be found in the section of the Bibliography headed *Teaching Approaches*. Among them, John Hodgson's *Improvisation*, Pemberton-Billing's *Teaching Drama* and Brenda Walker's *Teaching Creative Drama* have particularly helpful advice. Christopher Parry's *The Mummery* gives a fascinating account of work in drama undertaken in a specially adapted classroom. A useful anthology of extracts will be found in Reeves and Culpan's *Dialogue and Drama*.

4

Drama and the Scripted Play

THE PROCESS OF PREPARATION FOR PERFORMANCE

It is a sober commentary upon school drama, particularly the school play, when past students' most vivid recollections are of near-disasters, of plays provoking ill-timed hilarity rather than the remembrance of truly dramatic experiences. Numerous reasons exist for this situation, ranging from directorial incompetence to ventures undertaken for entirely wrong reasons. Fund raising and end of term frolics may be admirable activities but their relationship to drama is dubious. School drama as represented by the performance of scripted plays should be notable for its truly dramatic excitement rather than for boredom or catastrophe.

Ideally a play performance should develop from an existing pattern rather than occurring as an isolated incident. N. Caslin in *Creative Dramatics in the Classroom* makes a useful distinction by describing 'creative dramatics', i.e. drama within the educational programme, as 'the process', and 'Theatre', i.e. in this context the school play, as the 'product'. Successful and valuable dramatic experience by the children is more likely to be gained from a school play if it represents a culmination of their previous dramatic experience. Some teachers will feel that it is not an experience valuable to *all* children. Involvement should be an expression of continuing interest rather than external pressure

The production of a scripted drama will almost inevitably be a joint product by staff and pupils. One of its great benefits (sometimes recognised retrospectively) is the shared experience to which staff and children alike are exposed. There is no question of 'them' and 'us'. Co-operation and mutual understanding between teacher and pupil must exist for anything genuinely creative to take place. Few other school activities include this particular facet of relationships to such an extent. The children see the teacher facing his own problems that directly relate to their common enterprise. He possesses no secret answer book. Each production creates its own problems and opportunities to which a response is required not in terms of pupil/teacher but of dramatic integrity. This relationship is most likely to be successful if it develops from already established trust and respect.

Only the foolhardy or experienced teacher undertakes production of a full-length play. It is difficult to write a commentary appropriate to both. However a number of issues are inescapable. Basic decisions involve What? Where? When? and At what cost? It is easy to avoid answering these questions but at some point they become unavoidable, and it is best to take account of them as early as possible.

The answer to 'What' should almost certainly be 'something worth while'. An immense amount of effort and patience is going to be expended and it is not sensible to expend it on the third rate. Rather than waste attention on a poor play, teachers should make up their own scripts. They may have defects but at least they will have an element of creativity absent from the superficial commercial script. A play of quality will survive quite rough handling, whereas a play depending chiefly upon the sophisticated skills of a professional performer may well leave the amateur stranded. Sometimes a play is presented simply as a fund-raising activity. This is a thoroughly bad principle, since decisions are made for wrong reasons. The general guide-line should be: here is a play we think is worth performing and we hope the audience will share and enjoy the experience with us. The audience should be respected rather than indulged.

'Where?' There may be an obvious answer, but it should not be assumed too quickly that the school hall stage is the best and only place. It is not impossible to consider presenting the play in a number of locations to different audiences. Local community centres, other schools, church halls, may be suitable venues. A very vital experience is gained by working in different situations. If a tour is involved this must be considered from the start. Even in your own school environment, the stage may be unsuitable and other arrangements should be considered. But a decision on the space must be made early so that the technical planning can proceed effectively. The space must be large enough to accommodate your play, allow reasonably easy access and be capable of being viewed fairly comfortably by the audience.

The dates of performance should be fixed in good time so that everyone knows their commitment. Some form of budgeting is better than hopeful bankruptcy. Often, money raised with immense difficulty is squandered in thoughtless last minute expenditure which early planning could have avoided.

Preliminary planning is essential even if it is contrary to the director's temperament. It is perhaps worth while looking at a theatre programme to see how many people other than the actors are needed to present a play. It is fatal to assume that the producer will undertake all those tasks efficiently, hoping 'it will be all right on the night'. Most successful productions are the result of a team effort and assistance should be sought from colleagues early rather than late. Some will readily help, others will have to be cajoled, but their support is vital. It is a fact to be faced that the director will have to organise colleagues as well as the pupils. It will be a test of tact, patience and diplomacy. But any goodwill gained will be very valuable in future activities, whilst animosity will create the reverse effect. If colleagues can be persuaded to undertake named tasks rather than offer general help, the path will be easier. Where children are responsible for, or assisting, backstage activities, they and their jobs should be clearly identified. It is important to remember that a child's experience is limited and he should not be given too onerous a task without some tactful support. Tasks that must be handled are: stage-management and crew, prompt, scenery and property construction, costume design and construction, lighting, make-up, front of house arrangements, seating, publicity, invitations, sale and distribution of tickets, ushering, programme printing and distribution, photographs, overall business managements, and in larger enterprises, sale of refreshments, cloakroom facilities and car parking.

There is no single prescribed method of approach to production. Each director has his own way, but it is important that his approach is understood. The director should have a clear notion of the particular qualities of the play. He should give some thought to an analysis of its structure and style. It is hoped that he will respect the playwright's intention (this presupposes he recognises it) and will create a style of presentation that whilst being personal and individual will not entirely corrupt the original. Interpretation in terms of meaning, acting and costume style is inevitable. It is best if interpretation relates to a general scheme rather than exhibit diverse idiosyncrasies of acting, costume design and scenic devices. A good deal of unnecessary chafing is caused when members of the group do not really know what is expected of them. The director must be prepared to explain his approach and gain the confidence of the group. A cold direct confrontation with a difficult text is unlikely to be successful so that organisation of early rehearsals is particularly important. The overall shape of the play should never be destroyed by excessive attention to one aspect to the detriment of the other elements of the production. Working chronologically through the text scene by scene is not always the best. It is helpful to establish meaningful units that identify the relationships of the characters and how they fit together.

All this is best thought about before rehearsals begin. One of the best insurances for establishing confidence with a cast is the ability to answer their questions or direct their search to finding their own answers. This requires a good deal of preliminary work by the director in clarifying ideas in *his* own mind concerning the line of argument or the alternatives within the text. A model stage or stage plans are often helpful in elucidation and assist the technical staff to work with some independence.

Perhaps one of the major difficulties is casting. Choices have to be made and an element of competition may enter with resulting disappointment. The best plays to choose are those having a smallish cast of principals and a largish supporting cast. However the guiding rule should be 'the play's the thing'. A real help in removing a feeling of lacking opportunities is to plan a series of productions so that in time most who wish to will have a chance. To choose a play simply because it has a large cast is not desirable. If the cast includes a mixture of staff and pupils there is a special need for care in rehearsal and problems can arise. To give opportunity for performance to as large a number of people as possible alternates or understudies should be appointed whenever possible.

Rehearsals

It should be possible to produce some kind of schedule so that individuals can see their commitments. Actors tend to be very impatient waiting for their part of the play to be rehearsed and it is best to reduce that waiting time to the minimum. Of course delays cannot be eliminated and performers must know this. A chart noting individual character appearances with page numbers and text references will help to plan rehearsals to the best effect and use the time most economically. It is essential that rehearsals are lively and interesting. The atmosphere should be bright and enjoyable. Shouting and sarcasm are best avoided. Inevitably tense situations will arise in which the director's patience and skill are severely tested. It must be remembered that creativity does not occur in an atmosphere of tension caused by anger or bad temper. Creative tension is the confronting of a problem and searching energetically for its solution. Concentration and absorption are qualities to be developed since they will lead to the most rewarding rehearsal.

Problems of interpretation often bring rehearsals to an awkward halt with neither producer nor performer satisfied with what is being done. Often, the failure is to understand sufficiently *precisely*, so that further explanation is necessary. Discussion in terms of the particular character rather than vague generalised motivation is usually most satisfactory. Improvisation often clarifies the true situation or reveals where the misunderstanding lies. The director should constantly search for analogies within the pupils' experience. Carefully worded *questions* to the actor will often produce a more stimulating response than a carefully worded *direction*. Rather than allowing a single difficulty to hold up the whole proceedings, individual problems should be dealt with in private sessions. It is helpful if there is some sense of accomplishment at the end of each rehearsal and the director should remain perennially optimistic.

As the rehearsals proceed, costumes, properties and scenic effects should be introduced so that the performers become familiar with their use. The last-minute appearance of props can be very off-putting to the actor and reduce his performance to a struggle to accommodate a new feature of his costume or equipment. A number of dress rehearsals is really necessary if the technical effects are to be polished. A good deal of patience is needed at this point since lighting and stage technicians will have had far less rehearsal than performers. The backstage crew may be carrying out extremely complicated processes that need time and repetition to master. The actors should be reminded of this. Details of running time and length of intervals must be communicated to the front of house manager so that the audience may be informed. The final dress rehearsal should be as much like an actual performance as possible. It is usually valueless to attempt any adjustments after this point.

On the day or evening of the presentation the aim should be to begin at the advertised time. This implies a general agreement on time and the synchronisation of watches front of house and backstage. Performers should be made up and costumed in good time. Ideally the director should be free from any direct responsibility during the performance. In fact, the stage manager is in charge of the proceedings. Having given a few words of encouragement, the director is best advised to stay out of the way. From his observations during rehearsals, the stage manager will have devised a schedule of scenery changes and general timing, together with a call list for the actors who should stay away from the stage area until called. The stage manager and the house manager need to work out a careful plan for the actual opening so that neither is caught unawares. The arrangements will vary according to the conditions, but plans for warning bells, extinguishing lights in the auditorium, dealing with late-comers, length of intervals and time of the final curtain must be made. It is also very important that fire precautions are very strictly observed and that first aid equipment is to hand. Members of the audience do occasionally faint, trip, cough or otherwise disrupt the proceedings.

There is always a great sense of achievement and relief at the conclusion of a successful performance. Care should be taken to thank all those involved, return items that have been borrowed. Care at this point will reap dividends later. Conversely carelessness or disregard can create serious future problems. Any remaining enthusiasm should be devoted to planning future productions. The final performance may be disappointing or the audience unappreciative. Very careful consideration should be given to the reasons. The value to the pupils should not be discounted. The whole objective was to involve, interest them in a dramatic venture. They may readily accept the analogy of the football team losing, but nevertheless having had a worth-while game.

Since play production is a very complex business, this chapter necessarily surveys only general problems. A director should add to his own experience by reading about the problems and approaches to direction, and study in detail any approach with which he finds himself in sympathy. He will gain most experience by practical involvement.

Advice on play direction can range from the brief but cogent remarks found in the Women's Institute booklet *Focus on Drama* to the erudite and professional world contained in Stanislavski's *My Life and Art*. Style in direction is so personal that no single book is likely to provide a model for procedure and interpretation. It is therefore important to read widely and notice what facets of production are most frequently given prominence. You will then have to select ideas that approximate to you and your own particular situation. Techniques in dealing skilfully with technical problems are well worth acquiring, but the really imaginative creative director will always be searching for new ideas and trying out different forms of production. It is important not to settle into a comfortable routine method. John Fernald's *The Play Produced* is an introduction to the techniques of producing plays and makes an orderly examination of the whole process. He deals with dramatic contrasts in speech, movement, grouping as well as interpretation. His later book *Sense of Direction* represents an extension and enlargement of the earlier work. John Allen in *Play Production* denies that his book is a manual on the theory and practice of play production, but it carefully examines interpretative and creative aspects. A useful appendix suggests a programme for rehearsals. Peter Chilver and Eric Jones have written a group of books, *Staging the School Play, Designing the School Play* and *Make-Up for the School Play*, which deal with all the important features of preparation and presentation in a straightforward way. You may not, however, agree with some of the views expressed. Richard Courtney has also produced a helpful handbook *The School Play*. There is a host of books by professional directors which make fascinating reading. A useful collection of professional views will be found in Toby Chinoy's *Directors on Directing*. Two books by James Roose Evans, *Directing a Play* and *Experimental Theatre from Stanislavski to Today*, give some excellent and well-illustrated insights into the problems of directing.

5

Drama and the Theatre

Perhaps the situation can be best described by referring to three examples. The first occurred at a Stratford-upon-Avon production of *A Midsummer Night's Dream* where a large and noisy group of secondary school children completely ruined enjoyment of the play for any member of the audience sitting near them. Their chatter was incessant. Programmes and sweet papers fluttered continually and the fidgeting was generally very irritating. Their response had very little relevance to the play. The performance was of high quality. At what was considered an outstanding production of *The Three Sisters* at the National Theatre, I was impressed by the total absorption of a group of secondary schoolboys sitting in front of me. No head seemed to move and there were no whispered conferences. At a special schools performance of *Macbeth*, half the audience had been in the theatre during the day, discussing the play with the actors and director. The other half had not, and it was from the latter that the majority of distractions arose during a somewhat uneven production.

It seems clear that if the theatre visit is regarded as an outing a special treat or a compulsory excursion the motive is the wrong one. Certainly the Inspector of Taxes regards theatre visiting as a frivolous activity as one discovers when the cost of theatre tickets is laughingly excluded from professional expenses. Perhaps it is unfortunate that drama is such an enjoyable activity. If it were dull and boring, perhaps it would be considered more acceptably 'educational'. None the less theatre visiting is an extremely valuable educational experience if it is undertaken with the right motives and in the right spirit. Michael Billington in *Flourish*, the Royal Shakespeare Company newspaper (Summer 1971), presented an article, 'Teenage Critics', which consisted of a cross-section of essays written by secondary pupils after their visits to Stratford or the Aldwych Theatre. The comments, which revealed a very wide spectrum of responses and interests, related to detailed observations concerning stage setting and particular lighting effects, remarks on acting style and skill as well as the effect of the play itself. One girl referred to the squeaky seats and another detected the distinct difference in the atmosphere at a matinée performance for school children compared with a performance at which the majority of the audience were 'experienced theatre-goers'. She complained about a lack of audience participation at the matinée.

These comments illustrate that the interest of the children does extend into the many facets of theatre, acting, technical features of lighting and design, director's interpretation, comparisons of performances, e.g. 'Much better than the Nottingham *Ophelia*', the theatre building and the whole feeling of theatrical presentation. Wherever a special interest is expressed in a particular aspect, the lead should be followed up with those pupils.

Theatre-going might be part of a liberal education where numerous outside visits to museums, galleries, courts, factories, cinemas, theatres, display centres are arranged. The theatre visit is then seen in a sense of proportion with the focus on the particular visit rather than an occasion for an outing. In visiting a factory, one is interested in the product and the special design of the building in which it is being produced. Equally, a theatre visit is to a play *and* to a specialised building. Some information about how the theatre functions, perhaps a visit backstage will help to make the excursion more worth while. Those who feel that such visits ruin the 'magic' of the theatre will clearly not arrange them.

A theatre visit should have a real connection with what is being studied in the English and drama scheme of work. It is wrong to expect a group of children or fairly young adolescents to respond in an adult manner to a play which is not really intended for child audiences. Some preparation must be undertaken. Children should have some notion of what they are going to see, and of the style of presentation, e.g. whether they are merely spectators or involved actively in the performance. With a play that is very familiar to him personally the teacher may have forgotten the effect of the initial impact. Many programmes include only the briefest notes of the characters with very inadequate information concerning locations or settings. Indeed there seems to be an underlying assumption, particularly concerning Shakespearian productions, that everyone in the audience has seen the play before. There are admirable but expensive exceptions to this general rule. The more the children are prepared the more likely the visit is to be successful. It is important not to destroy the dramatic and theatrical effect of the play. There is no need to reveal the whole plot, or to describe a particular highlight. The best method, depending on the age of the children, is to create a sense of expectation and inquisitive interest. With youngsters it may be dropping a hint, with older pupils there might be queries about characterisation, interpretation or the style of the production. They might try out scenes for themselves and then compare the effect with what is seen at the theatre. The whole intention is to avoid a purely recreational attitude (enjoyment must be taken for granted) and to excite a deeper interest in the play and its realisation on the stage. Some theatres offer workshop sessions before or after performances and these are usually attractive. It must be remembered that directors and actors are not necessarily trained teachers and that their style of discussion may sometimes seem eccentric and casual – not in their own professional terms, but in relation to an uninitiated audience.

A theatre visit is a very risky business even at best. The quality of the performance may remain a largely unknown factor. All the organisational difficulties of transport, tickets, timing, food, toilet facilities must be efficiently dealt with. Every scrap of information must be gathered ranging from the collections of press reviews, theatre brochures and photographs to the location of the toilets and bus park. A preliminary visit by the teacher is one of the best insurances if it can be arranged. Every encouragement should be given to older pupils, either by themselves or in small groups, to make independent theatre visits. Teachers should investigate possibilities very carefully so that advantages from seat concessions and travel subsidies can be gained.

A reverse process, almost as risky, is the invitation to a theatre group to visit the school. It can be a very stimulating and productive occasion. The inexperienced teacher should be given an excellent, enlightening introduction to educational drama. Useful insights can be gained into teaching techniques. Ideas are acquired concerning the use of space. Children's responses to a skilled team familiar with the school situation using methods refined from their own previous experience can be observed. The visiting group will have had the opportunities to concentrate on their production, devising costumes and properties. They will have had time to research for materials and rehearse and test their approach. The individual members are likely to have acting *and* teaching skills. Their programme will relate closely to the age range of the audience and the particular environment. The group will also be able to respond directly to the audience, adjusting and developing their material, encouraging and involving the children. The warmth and excitement engendered by a good theatre group is very valuable. It can give a sense of richness and purpose.

Almost everything depends upon the quality of the theatre group. A teacher should acquaint himself with their work before extending an invitation. The effectiveness of the groups varies tremendously. Their reception into a school will almost certainly require substantial changes of timetable and reorganisation. Financial costs might be quite high. Colleagues in adjoining classrooms will welcome prior warning of a visit. The assessment of the total value to a school of a visiting theatre group is a complex and difficult process. Many teachers have welcomed such groups finding the sessions beneficial and stimulating to their own work. Such a visit might well open up an approach to drama not previously attempted.

E

It is well to find out details of the exact content and timing of the programme, how the group intend to organise their session especially when these involve classroom activities. The need for hall space and changing accommodation and audience seating arrangements, the placing of intervals must be considered. Almost always break-times and possibly meal-times have to be adjusted and the visitors will welcome some refreshment. Teachers should take the opportunity for observation and participation, of seeing how their own children respond to a different set of adults. They should create a sympathetic interest in what is being attempted. They should be ready to discuss the programme, assess the effectiveness of the presentation and handle any 'follow-up' suggestions.

The teacher's observations during a visit should take account of at least the following:

The material. Notice if the story or incident, is mundane, cliché-ridden or stereotyped, filled out with undifferentiated stock figures, or is given characters with lively individuality. For example, does a witch ever show characteristics that are not black, wicked and ugly? The overall shape of the play should be observed and note taken of whether it arrives at a satisfactory absorbing end or concludes in a dull and vague way with the dissipation of the children's interest.

Language. Assess the effectiveness of the language and style of speech. Some forms of improvisation produce a degenerate and dull style of speech which contribute nothing to language development.

Children. Observe how the children are invited to participate. Are they questioned directly or invited by imaginative involvement of which they are hardly conscious? The teacher should note carefully, though unobtrusively, how individual children respond. He will know the children far better than the performers and might get some surprises.

Use of space. It is unlikely that a children's theatre group will perform on a stage even if it is offered. Most frequently the play will be acted in a space in the centre of the hall with the children sitting on the floor round the edge of the space. The group usually gives considerable thought to the organisation and adaptation of that space and they may well offer useful suggestions which you may subsequently utilise. It should be noticed how the children are prevented from encroaching on the space. Methods of denoting locale, arrangement for scene and costume changes should also be noted. The players are establishing a concept of drama both in approach and realisation and the teacher should be ready to develop that concept if he thinks it valid.

Properties and costume. Many groups demonstrate a great deal of imagination in the devising and construction of their costumes and properties. A travelling group must inevitably work with a very limited wardrobe. They will refine their needs to the minimum consonant with effectiveness. The teacher should notice the kinds of costume that establish human, animal or imaginary characters with a speedy effectiveness and how properties that have to withstand a good deal of hard wear and tear are constructed. Particular items of costume or property that provoke or instigate the most dramatic interest should be identified for future reference.

Follow-up work. The theatre group may make suggestions or even carry out some of this work themselves, but the teacher should compile a list for himself as the visit proceeds. The work need not necessarily be drama. Indeed it would be probably inviting cliché or superficial imitation to suggest activities too closely paralleled by the work that they have seen. The value lies elsewhere. First the energising effect of a good group may stimulate work in drama for the first time. It would not be sensible to copy what is, in fact, a complicated, carefully organised, rehearsed process. Perhaps during the performance other stories, poems or episodes suggested themselves for dramatic treatment. One of the characters might have been so vivid that the class could invent another adventure for him. The children might like to construct some of the properties or make paintings, models or puppets of particular scenes. They might write their own stories and descriptions. It is important not to make heavy weather of any follow-up work so that the excitement engendered by the visit is destroyed. This is fatal. Rather should the visit be used as a springboard for class activities or as a reference point when later in a drama lesson the solution to a problem may be seen by recalling the theatre group visit.

PROFESSIONAL THEATRE

In recent years, there has been a welcome and increasing interest shown by the professional theatre in their contact with young people. The range of activities offered is indeed extensive and many different categories exist within the range. Included will be (i) the presentation of plays from the normal repertoire; (ii) plays or musicals specially selected and aimed at a young audience; (iii) plays specially written for young people of a particular age range; (iv) programmes devised from the dramatisation of literary, historical, scientific materials often of a documentary nature; (v) puppet plays; (vi) dance drama and ballet; (vii) mime.

In the first category, the Royal Shakespeare Company provides some useful examples. Certain 'club' performance of plays in the repertory are presented and it is possible for teachers to obtain group membership for their pupils. Membership of the club brings certain price and booking concessions of which many schools already take advantage. The Young Vic gives an idea of the second category. It is important to note, however, that the general public is not excluded from the performances and there is no sense of 'playing down' to the audience. Titles such as *Oedipus Rex* or *Waiting for Godot* in one programme of plays are sufficient to squash that view. The same season included a farce, *Scapino*, and a multi-media rock musical, *Stomp*. A number of professional companies throughout the country adopt a similar kind of policy. The teacher should make himself familiar with what is available locally, especially where national companies operate tours or include a touring section such as the Royal Shakespeare's Theatregoround, which arranges performances in schools or colleges. Shakespeare, Shaw and contemporary playwrights appear to be given most frequent performances.

Sometimes plays are written especially for young audiences with a specific age range in mind. At the upper end are plays such as Peter Terson writes for the National Youth Theatre and in this particular case acted by young performers. Caryl Jenner's Unicorn Theatre has productions aimed, though not exclusively, at audiences below fourteen years of age. There is a certain skill in writing plays for children that not all playwrights possess, however competent they may be at the adult level. The teacher may need to exercise some caution before exposing the children to these plays which range from the brilliant to the mediocre. Personal visits or scrutiny of reviews is important.

Several companies specialise in devising programmes that move outside the format of the straightforward play. Such titles as 'Cuts and Cruises', a programme about Inland Waterways, and 'Living Cathedral', a study of Lincoln Cathedral, identify attempts to explore ideas of local interest and use geographical or social information related to a particular neighbourhood. The Theatre in the Round, Stoke on Trent, has pioneered projects of this kind. The Greenwich Theatre produced a musical play, not specifically for youth audiences but nevertheless appropriate, *Down the Arches*, which told of the planning of an ambitious railway scheme in South-East London. Work that began experimentally, but through experience has grown into a strong, well-developed concept is Coventry's Theatre in Education, supported by the local authority, but based at the Belgrade Theatre. Their projects are far from simple, spanning several weeks with the actor/teachers working in schools. There is an emphasis upon research and fact-finding and the utilisation, frequently in documentary drama, of the findings that have been extracted and discussed. Topics have included 'The Industrial Revolution' and 'War in Literature'. The group have evolved a method of pupil participation that includes research, discussion, improvisation and play-making in a thoughtful and sensitive combination.

The whole idea of documentary drama is very much alive at present and useful hints on materials and procedures can be gleaned that might be appropriate in the teacher's own school or classroom drama.

Puppet plays tend to adhere to traditional material re-enacting old legends and fairy tales. Russian stories seem to be particularly popular. The appeal is usually to younger audiences. It is worth noting that puppetry in other European countries, notably Poland and Czechoslovakia, is much more sophisticated and includes programmes for adults as well as children. Tours are often arranged by professional companies. These visiting companies, such as the Paper Bag Players of New York, exhibit extraordinary talent, but sometimes the strangeness of the material and different conventions prevent their skill from being fully appreciated by the child audiences.

A few dance companies exist which tour schools and colleges. Some employ traditional dance techniques while others, like the British Dance Drama Theatre, are based on modern dance methods. These programmes take in a wide range of age groups and often include spoken drama, music, poetry and experimental work in sound and light. Also found are solo performers who present programmes of dance, mime, poetry or drama.

In most of the examples given so far the young audiences have been engaged principally as viewers. Some professional companies adopt a different approach which involves participation and physical involvement by the children during the performance. A good deal of exciting experimental work has been carried out particularly by Brian Way at the Theatre Centre. Indeed the aim of that centre is 'to provide opportunities for experiment and research into forms of theatre most suitable for children of all ages'. The plays are specially written but do not resemble the orthodox script, neither do the rehearsal or actor/audience techniques. The actors may first work with groups of children in their own classrooms devising properties and costumes as well as working on sections of the story. Later they become involved as participants, as observers or in discussion groups. One programme, 'Three Faces', devised by Brian Way, has a play, 'Balloon Faces', for infants which is a story of a little girl and a balloon. For juniors, 'Magical Faces' tells the story of a town in which no one is allowed to laugh and for top juniors, 'Adventure Faces' concerns the adventures of a carnival king and his family. The audience participation includes movement, improvising musical instruments and sounds and mask making. Suggestions for follow-up work are made by the Company and it is possible to hire or buy kits that contain very detailed information.

This concept of drama in education does not have the whole-hearted support of all teachers. Many feel that the particular excitement and magic of the theatre experience is lost and that often the children's activities are trivial or crude. They believe that the presentation of a traditional play is more enjoyable for the children. Of course neither form is exclusive. The teacher should take advantage of attending any performances he can in order to make a reasonable judgement. Basically the question to be asked is 'What is the nature of the experience that you wish the children to have?'

Perhaps it is worth mentioning at this point some of the more extremely adventurous child participatory drama that moves completely away from the ordinary dramatic and theatrical modes, yet in a sense reverts back to one of the earliest dramatic excursions – the procession of celebration with song and dance. A leading exponent is an American, Ed Berman, who conducts his activities as often in the street as inside a building. The work conceives of drama as play or a game in a community situation. An immense vigour underlies the work which, unfettered by any rigid script may build up from a procession through the streets of a group of boldly costumed figures – they have included moonmen and comic book heroes – and an open-ended game develops from the interaction between the troupe and the bystanders. Activities include painting, modelling, designing, music making. The whole object is to inject feeling, responsiveness and community action into areas such as housing developments of high sky-scraper blocks where hard, uninviting play areas seem devoid of colour or interest. Teachers may find some of their children becoming involved in such groups and carrying through their interest into classroom activities. Some may even feel bold enough to try a local experiment.

The National Youth Theatre, planned, developed and directed by Michael Croft epitomises his view of what youth theatre should be. Now permanently housed in the Shaw Theatre in Euston Road with the professional Dolphin Theatre Company, the programme of plays whilst following a somewhat more formal pattern of theatre presentation remains sensitive and aware of the young audience. Recently the repertoire has included *Slip Road Wedding*, an adaptation by Peter Terson of Lorca's *Blood Wedding*, Willis Hall's *The Long and the Short and the Tall* and a children's play *The Plotters of Cabbage Patch Corner*. As well as the professional company's presentations, the National Youth Theatre's own productions with young people continue. These include Shakespeare and contemporary plays. Michael Croft holds very strong views on drama and theatre in relation to education which do not correspond with other leading advocates. He would dispute, for example, the primacy of improvisation. The years of struggle through which Michael Croft has persevered indicate the strength and persistence of the vision of drama he possesses. Teachers need to make their own assessment of the work, preferably after a visit to the Shaw Theatre or to a travelling group from N.Y.T.

Local theatres that do not have extensive plans for work in educational drama may still have clubs for young play-goers where Saturday or holiday sessions are presented for interested children to attend and participate.

With all this range of possibilities of activities and visits, what is the class teacher to do? First there must be a careful assessment and evaluation of the possibilities so far as his particular school is concerned. He will obtain as much detailed information as possible by gathering brochures of different companies, programmes of local or regional theatres. Whenever possible he should make personal visits, garner impressions from colleagues and teachers at other schools whilst allowing for personal preferences and prejudices. He should try to see how visits to the school or theatre trips will relate to his own work in drama so that the value will be maximised. This implies careful preparation and follow-up work. Sometimes the companies will provide assistance but often the teacher must plan his own projects. Care must be taken not to destroy or devalue the experience that the children undergo by making associated projects dull and unadventurous. Ensuing activities might relate only indirectly to the actual performance. The teacher might discover some ideas about costume and design which he can use on a future occasion. He might find out new ways of utilising the classroom shapes. He might be stimulated in his search for dramatic material or projects in improvisation or play-making. Though the teacher will wish to know the children's impression of a visiting company or theatre performance, reports, comments or essay type work should be generally avoided. It is the *activity* of drama that should be stimulated and developed.

Perhaps one of the major problems in arrangements for theatre trips or visiting companies is finance. The teacher should discuss with his head teacher what funds are available or how they might be raised. Costs can sometimes be reduced by using the school as a centre and sharing a visit with another school. Financial discussion will only be meaningful if the cost is realistically assessed. However it is cheering to note that when tour programmes of theatre companies are examined many schools do find a successful solution to the financial problems.

Even if the teacher can arrange no visits to his school it should not be impossible for him to make personal visits to theatrical activities which might serve to spark off ideas for lessons and projects. In this work it is essential constantly to search for refreshment and enlightenment.

The National Council of Theatre for Young People publishes regular bulletins announcing plans of forthcoming productions from Theatre in Education groups. Some Companies publish very full individual pro-grammes and reports of their activities (examples are contained in the Appendixes). In the spring of 1970, *New Theatre Magazine* devoted an entire issue to 'Drama and Young People'. In another issue of the same publication (vol. XI, no. 1) Tim Appelbee describes 'Summer Street Theatre for Children' and David Illingworth 'The Bristol Street Theatre Troupe: a do-it-yourself kit'. *Drama in Theatre and Education* contains an article by Mark Woolgar on 'The Professional Theatre in and for Schools'.

6

Drama and the Arts

ART AND CRAFT

Whilst drama shares an oral and aural interest with English, visually it has much in common with art. Drama is a 'seen' activity. It makes use of arrangement of space – the 'virtual' space of Susanne Langer applies both to drama and to art. The organisation of the dramatic space has similarities with the artists' concern for composition. Both give consideration to line and colour. A picture may be called 'dramatic' because of its vigorous focus upon a physical attitude, a strong block of colour, a set of vivid contrasts or subtle use of light effects. In three dimensional, plastic art, the sculptor reveals the same concern for form and movement as does the director or actor. In scenic design, costume and lighting, the relationship is immediate and direct.

As the artist creates within the discipline of his material, striving to give form to an inwardly felt impulse, so in the drama a similar process takes place, more complex because of the complexity of the activity where the creative expression includes author, director, actor. Though the art of drama is temporary and transient and the artist's presentation is direct and permanent, aspects of the creative process remain remarkably similar.

In drama the playwright creates the environment of the action. Usually a three-dimensional space is envisaged with the performers contained within that environment. Although three-dimensional, the stage space is not real, it uses a series of conventions which the audience is invited imaginatively to accept. In recent times that space, having escaped the restrictions of the proscenium arch, has become more plastic, less precisely defined, but it still depends upon the same appeal to the imagination that the Chorus makes in *Henry V*. Artists may often seek for a three-dimensional effect on their canvases by careful use of perspective, or in choice of tones or colours or surface treatment. Both artist and playwright are aware that the imaginative identification by the viewer of that space in naturalistic or abstract terms is a vital factor. Although now rather old fashioned, the term 'willing suspension of disbelief' is apposite. Within the total space is a whole set of spatial relationships created by objects or figures. A recognition of the potency, subtlety and power created by the sensitive arrangement of those related objects is important in art and drama even though the final objectives of the two arts remain distinct and separate. The pliability, character and form of the individual shapes are themselves intriguing whether as objects within a still life group or as stage figures. In a sense, Dame Laura Knight's circus pictures are theatrical 'still lifes'. The attitude of the body, the droop of the head, the facial expression, the juxtaposition of colour, the line and texture inspire to a picture in one direction and create a circus performance in another. As the picture transcends the actual objects it depicts, becoming something of unique and individual existence, so the actor on the stage seeks to expose a deeper and more subtle meaning than the surface reality. Both reach beyond the photographic or representational.

When we consider set design, costume and lighting, then the common visual ground should be readily recognised, though there is often a reluctance in educational drama to consider the importance of the visual effects to the total aesthetic impression. The phrase 'backstage' when applied to set builders and painters, and dress-makers is unfortunate. The results of their efforts are anything but backstage. They can make or mar the dramatic offering. It may well be that for a teacher or a particular class of children that an approach to drama is successfully achieved through work in art and a teacher should feel no compunction in adopting this approach. Any skill or sensitivity acquired can make a rich and exciting contribution to drama.

That drama has always had a persistent concern with space is obvious when one examines the development of the playing space in theatres and the current controversies related to stage shapes. Richard Southern's *The Seven Ages of the Theatre* or Stephen Joseph's *New Theatre Forms* usefully trace the historic development and contemporary issues. A drama production takes over the existing space whether it is the village green or grand opera house and transforms it into another environment suitable for a particular play. The organisation of the space, its limits and dimensions, raises practical, dramatic and aesthetic considerations. Books illustrating stage settings will show the extremely varied responses to organising that space. They will include attempts to recreate a real environment down to the minutest details, great perspective scenes achieved by series or flats and painted backcloths as well as abstract forms and shapes that have no immediately identifiable location.

It is important that no conventional solution is assumed for staging and designing either school productions or less formal dramatic ventures. The director and designer should start from the empty space and not feel bound by any existing drapes or stage arrangements. Part of the creativity of drama lies in the imaginative organisation of the acting space. The issue is threefold: the shape of the space, the way it is divided up and the selection of colours, textures, patterns for the surfaces that are exposed. It is worth while allowing some free experiment with these basic problems by making box shapes rather like model stages, of various dimensions and trying different arrangements of structures, shapes and levels within the space and observing how the application of paint or surface texture enhances or detracts from the total effect. In realistic designs questions of perspective, accurate decoration and detail will be uppermost. In more abstract approaches, structures depending on mass, shape line and level may emerge that offer real dramatic potential. A model set for a play is, after all, the culmination of a series of experiments in dividing up a particular space and creating a colour scheme that combines costume and set into a coherent whole. The demand is both practical and aesthetic. What is designed must be capable of translation into actuality, but it should be more than merely functional. The more the designer works from the basis of space, and spatial relationships and colour, the less likely is he to employ rather superficial and traditional processes.

Colleagues teaching art may be willing to allow experiments to take place in their lessons, since these concepts have something in common with three-dimensional design and to a lesser extent in two-dimensional work such as painting. Although the painter has a completely different intention in mind, it is worth noting his concern with design and colour on the canvas. Many pictures having what might be called 'dramatic' qualities can be translated into terms of drama without being simply copied. Still life studies show a response to shape, colour and balance and these are of equal importance to the designer. Figure drawing takes account of body shape, attitudes, physical tensions and the relationship of the figure to its background or environment – so does the play director.

Perhaps the description of one or two experiments will illustrate the scope of work possible in this particular area. Working from a box with one side open and the interior painted black, pupils were invited to place arrangements of objects – small blocks, matchboxes, shaped clay, twisted wire, and to see the various effects gained by arranging them in different positions in the box and in different relations to each other. Various coloured materials were introduced and alternative types and colours of lighting were used for illumination. Several factors quickly emerged. The objects set up a relationship with the whole space and with each other giving, for instance, impressions of smallness or dominance. Also created was a sense of scale and within the contained space of the material such as twisted wire, another set of spatial relationships was introduced. Colour and light direction was obviously important and caused dramatic changes in the appearance of the objects as well as creating pools of darkness and shadow. The miniature scale of the materials made quick rearrangements or adjustment possible. The activity could be undertaken on a larger scale using acting blocks, steps, rostra or the rigid types of cardboard container. With these constructions painted and textured by the addition, for instance, of egg boxes or coarse fabrics, and illuminated with whatever lighting equipment is available, a real investigation of the ideas of stage design is instigated.

In another experiment, the students supplied with a large amount of variously coloured, semi-transparent tissue paper were invited to create, in abstract terms, a surface that suggested a particular mood chosen by themselves. Contrasting shapes and subtle arrangements of colours were obtained by choosing a dominating colour, and overlaying with different coloured tissues that complemented or extended the range of tones and tints. Later, these small-scale patterns were enlarged into screens which were used to create an environment in which physical action could take place. An estimate of the effectiveness of the original idea translated into practical stage units then became possible. These experiments required attention to be given to both aesthetic and practical considerations. In another experiment, inventiveness was tested by making available a strictly limited group of objects (e.g. two rostra and one set of steps) and exploring the number of arrangements that these objects allowed and discovering which of these created or contained a space that suggested dramatic possibilities. For example, two rostra six feet by three feet placed at right angles form a contained space, whilst placed end to end they make a barrier dividing the space. Much more subtle arrangements are, of course, possible and they should be explored. One group devised a setting using three six-foot by three-foot rostra and a set of steps that successfully allowed the staging of several scenes from *Hamlet* with the minimum of fuss.

The main objective is to create a recognition that drama takes place in a space and considerable aesthetic attention must be given to the organisation of that space. Where ideas are translated into reality, practical considerations become important. The space must be capable of being used by the actor, it must have means of access and the scenic features must be of sufficient strength to have stability, yet remain portable.

The most important feature arising from the concept of space organisation is the notion of design. Extremely simple arrangements may consist of a series of blocks and steps based on a rectilinear pattern. It will soon be discovered that the rectangular shape is not the most flexible or useful. Triangular, hexagonal and circular shapes are to be preferred since they allow a greater variety of shapes to emerge. Sets may require different acting levels or particular parts to have a special focus requiring vertical constructions as backing or support. At this stage, screens, flats, or curtains may be introduced. It is essential that they relate to the overall design concept and are not simply used for screening unwanted stage areas. In recent years much greater attention has been paid to the relationship of floor, wall and ceiling surfaces of the stage. The average school designer will not be able to emulate Peter Hall in ordering special metallic floor strips for his production of *The Wars of the Roses*, but he must remain conscious that a problem exists. With limited facilities, the simple coherent design, *carefully lighted* to exclude unwanted areas is probably preferable to an elaborate, illustrative decor of flats and curtains with miscellaneous decorative features. In a production of an opera seen in school recently, the smallish stage was crammed with performers and scenery and very little movement was possible. A solution in this case would have been for the audience to sit on the stage and for the performance to take place on the floor of the hall. Then a much more dramatically exciting performance could have taken place.

Designing the space is clearly allied to designing the costumes. Here again it is best to avoid conventional assumptions with the hiring or borrowing of costumes. Work in fabric printing and dyeing could well relate to costume design. Free experiment should precede specific costume design so that the imagination is stretched and opened up to new possibilities. Fabrics specially dyed or printed for a particular production are usually to be preferred to the smartest hired costumes that do not allow the particular and unique quality of a production to emerge. There are exceptions in which the tailoring and design requirements are beyond the skills of the pupils or staff seamstresses. As with scene design, all kinds of research is necessary for historical detail, significant styles and fashions of a particular period. Colour schemes must be devised and consideration given to the treatment of surfaces by pattern or texture. It cannot be stressed too firmly that the concept of design is just as important when the total stage and costume requirements consist of a few boxes and three lengths of dyed butter muslin or hessian as it is with the most complicated set and costume. Although the process becomes more complex, the basic concept remains unchanged.

Building sets and making costumes and properties demand both practical and aesthetic skills. The crafts associated with normal carpentry and dress making are not synonymous with the needs of theatrical stagecraft and costume construction. Since the aim is different, the process will be different. Sets and costumes have to resist temporarily extremely heavy wear and tear but they seldom have a permanent existence and the ability to dismantle them is important. A dress in one production may supply a skirt for one costume, a bodice for another and the sleeves for yet another on a future occasion. Sets that have an enviable solidarity yet resist the efforts of scene shifters are unsatisfactory. Materials and fabrics traditionally associated with carpentry and dress-making are frequently replaced by substitutes in polystyrene, hessian, string, latex, plastic glues and paint. A close examination of the costumes used in the television series *The Six Wives of Henry VIII* reveals the use of canvas, coarse lace sprayed with dye, curtain rings and picture chain in costumes of apparently richly jewelled brocade. These examples show the need for inventiveness in costume making and the necessity to recognise the peculiar needs of stage and costume design. It is substantially different from making furniture or garments used or worn in everyday life.

Inventiveness and skill is also required in the making of stage properties such as jewellery, crowns, rings, goblets, swords and shields and other unlikely objects that a production may demand. The introduction of plastics have revolutionised the making process. The papier mâché techniques have been superseded by new methods and new materials. A good deal of free exploration is necessary in using waste objects such as empty plastic containers, polystyrene scraps as well as plastic modelling materials and new adhesives, paints, sprays and dyes. Now materials can be textured and objects constructed that are both lightweight and capable of withstanding the heavy demands that are made on stage properties. Ideas of design can be extended to the properties if they are made for a particular production. The resulting effect is much better than that gained from miscellaneous objects collected from a variety of sources. Research into the characteristics of armour, jewellery, hairdressing of various historical periods becomes necessary for precise information. The process of translating a historical model into a theatrical property raises certain problems. Meticulous copying is seldom successful. The maker has to assess the particular qualities of the original and reproduce them in a simplified, stylised and often enlarged form. All stage design needs simplicity and boldness for maximum effect with a clear profile or silhouette, but still suggesting the special quality of the period represented.

Puppetry
Puppetry is an activity that has obvious connections with drama. The perennial appeal of Punch and Judy and of more recent television characters such as Dougal in *The Magic Roundabout* are good examples. The relationship is twofold. Puppets represent very vigorous, well-defined characters manipulated by hand or string. The features, costumes and movement together create a very strong impression. These same elements are those which an actor must consider in developing a character part. Secondly it is possible from the interaction of a group of puppets to develop little incidents from which situation and dialogue can be created. Too often, puppets made with considerable care and skill, are left suspended in the air or pinned on the wall as part of the classroom decoration, instead of being used to exploit their dramatic potential. This error can be

avoided if right from the start, the puppets, however simple in construction, are put into situations that demand action by the operators and conversation with other puppets. The approach to puppetry will vary according to the age range of the children, but with infant, and junior children, speed and vigour in construction and immediate utilisation is to be encouraged. More complex forms such as marionettes are best handled later. Ping-pong balls, paper bags, boxes, tubes, potatoes, plastic containers all readily create quite effective characters both human and non-human. With a ping-pong ball, a felt pen, scraps of crepe hair and a handkerchief, a lively puppet can be produced in a matter of minutes. The caps from washing-up liquid containers, pipe cleaners and potatoes can be combined to create weird animals and monsters. The variations and possibilities are tremendous. Sets of eyes, mouths, eyebrows, hair-pieces and moustaches can quickly create a range of characters from a single basic figure.

Having been made, the puppets should be activated, perhaps in meeting a strange animal or object. When confrontation or conflict occurs then a miniature drama develops. It is useful to allow the class to invent their characters quite freely and then to combine contrasting characters which offer exciting possibilities. If some kind of background is painted or built enclosing the acting space, then a miniature theatre is created. Large boxes or cartons make very useful supports. The dialogue may be spontaneous, improvised or scripted. The vocal aspect is of great interest. Children can use their gifts of mimicry and accent without feeling exposed which can be a boon to shy children and they improvise the dialogue through their puppets. The activity also encourages projection and audibility in a positive way. The reason for clarity becomes obvious. The teacher should observe carefully the kind of puppets that the children create. Any kings, queens, princes, knights, magicians or witches – all archetypal figures – can be used in story-telling sessions.

Some interesting work has developed recently in the creation of abstract puppets, i.e. objects having no obviously human form but providing contrasts in shape, colour and flexibility. New possibilities of manipulation are opened up with for example the discovery of the movement characteristics of parallelograms where the angles are joined. The ways this flexible figure relates to a group of bobbing multicoloured tennis balls on sticks allows unusually vivid dramatic situations to develop.

Masks

The mask has always been a part of the actor's equipment. In the earliest forms of Greek comedy and tragedy, the actor depended on masks to depict his character and temperament. Much of the bold characterisation of the *Commedia dell 'Arte* results from the very well-defined masks that certain of the characters wear and even modern playwrights such as Brecht,

Genet and Arden have written plays which include partially masked characters. Stage make-up is also concerned with making a flexible mask. Circus
clowns have refined this technique to create very individualised styles. A
great deal of mystery has always surrounded masks. Primitive religious
rites often include frightening masked dancers who imitate fierce gods or
dangerous animals. The teacher should be aware of the element of fear
associated with masks. It is necessary to be cautious in the introduction of
mask making especially with younger children. The activity can be
approached at a number of levels, but if the intention is to relate the work
to drama, then the masks must always be thought of in terms of being
worn so that the wearer can *see* and *move* in his mask. Anything that
restricts vision or activity is to be avoided. A start could be made by
using individual features, not unlike the comic items found in joke shops
such as goggle eyes, moustaches, beards, odd shaped noses, peculiar
glasses. The items might be made of scrap material or fashioned from
papier mâché or a newer flexible plastic material that can be softened and
moulded and then dried into a rigid form. It is well to have the improvisation box ready, with a supply of hats and cloaks or lengths of materials,
so that an accompanying costume can quickly be constructed. Scraps of
dialogue or speech should be encouraged as they are suggested by the final
effect. There could be a progression to half-masks, experiments with creating varieties of expression (Greek masks give good suggestions) with the
addition of hair and beards made from wigs, coarse wool, string, crepe
hair or plumber's tow. Stylised effects rather than realistic ones should be
sought. If possible, the remaining exposed part of the face should be
disguised with theatrical make-up. This activity offers a good opportunity
to try out new materials and styles. Teenage girls might be glad of the
chance to experiment freely with make-up. Headpieces such as crowns,
helmets and horns can be added and the costumes completed from the
improvisation box. Then whole masks might be attempted or perhaps
masks created by make-up alone.

One experiment that might be worth trying with older children who
have become confident in using masks is to begin with a blank oval-shaped
card covering the face and held in position with loops of elastic over the
ears. Gradually a character is developed, first by the addition of eye slits,
and then eyebrows, mouth, hair, beard, etc., using scraps of materials or
felt pens or, what is extremely effective, paper sculpture techniques. It is
incredible how the eye slit will set the style of the other features and give
an unusual insight into one of the aspects of characterisation. It is possible
to work towards masks demonstrating contrasting features, e.g. happy/sad,
strong/weak, with the obvious dramatic potential of the contrasting characters who are created. Certain plays, *The Caucasian Chalk Circle, Noah's
Flood, Happy Haven* require masks for some of the characters and other

dramatic stories – *The Man in the Iron Mask, Pinocchio, The Lion, the Witch and the Wardrobe* suggest very interesting characters that would respond to an approach through masks.

Many playwrights, notably Chekhov and Ibsen, set out to create very particular moods in their plays by specifying in great detail the furnishing and colouring of their sets. They are trying to evoke an impression or feeling that will reinforce the play's impact. This mood is created by a combination of effects important amongst which are colour and light. The search for colour schemes appropriate for feelings of happiness, sadness, gaiety or sombre moods is essentially aesthetic. It will soon be realised that simply to use black for sadness or sobriety quickly leads to an overall dullness and that much more subtle effects must be sought. The juxtaposition and layering of colours and textures all contribute. The shape and colour of the actual stage surface will need careful attention. It is useful when experimenting with stage construction or making model sets to attempt to create a design that gives a distinctive impression yet includes some subtleties of colouring or pattern that might be used in the costume design so that one relates to the other in a sensitive rather than obvious way. It is also important to make sets that can create very different impressions according to the light sources. The contrasting scenes of the palace and the sheep-shearing scenes in *The Winter's Tale* provide a problem when a quick change of mood is required without a great deal of time for stage adjustment.

The phrase 'being in the limelight' refers to the theatrical device that was once popular of flooding the main character with a bright light, the 'lime' refers to the type of light used and bothering little about the illumination of the other actors on the stage. Compared with the subtle use of light in Rembrandt's *The Night Watch* in which the main features stand out from the surrounding darkness, the theatrical device seems very crude. Fortunately, however, we have now gained a very precise and subtle control over lighting apparatus with spot and flood lights, dimming apparatus and means of colouring or tinting light sources. Most schools have very limited stage lighting equipment. Often what is installed is inappropriate or badly used. Lighting is one of the most valuable assets in drama and the teacher should familiarise himself with its use. The great mystery that is alleged to surround the technical aspects of lighting is largely fictitious and experience can be gained fairly painlessly. However limited the resources, the teacher must ensure that he is exploiting them to the full. Intense interest has been demonstrated in the use of light and its dramatic qualities as can be seen in *Son et Lumière* productions and the psychedelic light shows that have become so popular. The artist has always shown a concern for light and its effects. One has only to look at a Dutch interior or impressionist paintings. Lighting design has become recognised as a theatre art. The

F

exploration of the relationship between the two forms might lead to exciting discoveries and useful co-operation.

Pollock's Toy Theatre was a delight to many Victorian school children and the popularity of model theatres has persisted. The traditional settings and characters of the fairy-tales and romances have always evoked interest and delight. Children can be encouraged to construct their own models and create their own characters and settings to avoid a simply imitative exercise. The activity raises all the issues of design, costume, scenery, properties. The initial interest might be in the technicalities of the construction but with encouragement, model making can lead to genuinely creative work in design and even improvisation and script writing.

For precise information concerning the practical aspects of theatre crafts, the teacher must refer to the particularly large number of handbooks that exist. These explain in great detail aspects of design, lighting, costume and property making, scenery construction, stage management, make-up, puppetry and shadowgraphs. Teachers may be confused by the contradictory nature of some of the ideas suggested. This is an area in which a great deal of contention exists and differences are reflected in the attitudes of the writers. Stage shape, design and lighting attract particularly vociferous argument. There are so many books that it is difficult to construct a recommended short list. Perhaps it is possible to mention Irene Corey's *The Mask of Reality* which outlines an approach to design for theatre, Frederick Bentham's *The Art of Stage Lighting*. Sheila Jackson's *Simple Stage Costumes and How to Make Them*, Philippe Perrotet's *Practical Stage Make-up* and Michael Grater's *Paper Faces*. Full details of many other extremely helpful books are listed in the Bibliography.

MUSIC

Singing has much in common with speaking. There is a mutual concern with breath control and utterance. Singing adds refinements of tone and pitch to the speaking voice. Speech tune, especially in English, is fairly restricted, whilst tune in song is one of its most musical characteristics. Rhythm, intonation, emphasis, volume and phrasing play their part in both activities. Many dramatists have been quick to spot the almost magical quality of songs within drama. One need look no further than Shakespeare. *Twelfth Night*, for example, is full of songs.

Music when it becomes instrumental introduces another set of conventions peculiar to itself including rules of great complexity and organisation in terms of scales, chords, orchestration, etc. Musicians rightly become a little perturbed when they hear music introduced into drama with no regard for its quality and value as music. It is a very tricky problem relating music to drama. Mendelssohn's overture for *A Midsummer Night's Dream* has little dramatic connection with the play as it is now conceived. Greig's music for *Peer Gynt* led to sharp exchanges between the composer and Ibsen who found the music quite unsuitable for his play. It is important to respect the differences as well as to utilise the common features of the two arts. Of course, a great deal of music has been written for dancing not only in the popular and ballet idioms but in more classical compositions that had their origins in dance suites.

The common emphasis exists in a number of quite simple matters. We are aware that speech consists of a combination of percussive and pitched sounds emanating from the area of the mouth, nose and throat. The plosive and fricative clicks and hisses, though derived from a different source are not unlike the beats, scrapes and reverberations of percussion instruments. Degrees of loudness, variations of volume, juxtaposition of contrasting noises, use of silence or pause, the creation of sound patterns are the variables in percussive music and vocalisation. Experience in one activity may help highlight a feature of the other with an increase of aural awareness and sensitivity. Some, whose ears are insufficiently attuned, find ideas of pitch change in speech difficult to detect. The famous 'Rain in Spain' song from *My Fair Lady* is a neat adaptation of a speech tune into song and music. Simple pitched percussion instruments allow experiment and understanding to be acquired. Sequences of sounds representing the vocal components of sentences might be reflected in compositions using percussion and/or pitched notes.

The natural actions of the body – heartbeat, pulse, breathing, swing and stepping are sufficient to confirm that the body carries a whole set of inbuilt rhythms capable of considerable variety and change. We are aware of the racing pulse and the thudding heart, the held breath and the patterned march or swinging arms. In music there is an equally basic concern with rhythm. The physical response to music might be a tapping foot, a waltz, a war dance and the action frequently reflects the rhythmical element. But music is also capable of evoking an emotional response or creating a particular mood or atmosphere. There can be no doubt of its direct connection with physical and emotional responsiveness which is such an important part of drama, particularly in movement and dance. It is unnecessary to emphasise that music is a powerful and potentially dangerous medium as exemplified by the pounding war drum or the damaged hearing of certain pop group performers. It must therefore be handled with circumspection and catholicity. Music for movement, dance and drama should be carefully chosen but the range of selection should be extremely wide. Pop, jazz, light, classical, serious – all these forms have a contribution to make and, equally important, music making can have a substantial value in dramatic work.

Sea shanties and work songs are composed with a feeling for a particular rhythm related to a physical action. The capstan shanty differs from the rope-hauling song. The pattern is devised to facilitate and sustain action and the relationship is organic both in rhythm and words that almost inevitably reflect some aspects of the life at sea. The original compositions and collections of Ewan McColl, Peggy Seeger and Charles Parker are notable examples of work songs. Action songs written for children too often suggest contrived mechanical actions that are unimaginative and superficial. Action songs, if they are used at all, must have vitality and real meaning. Ballad singing, unaccompanied or with guitar often contributes directly to a dramatic idea. Brecht uses the device to great effect in his play *Mother Courage*. The songs in *Marat/Sade* make a powerful contribution to Peter Weiss's drama. It may well be that in play-making on either literary or documentary topics good use can be made of songs and ballads, perhaps in handling difficult narrative sequences or making comment on the action. The style is bold and direct and contrasts well with the spoken word. Plays such as *Oh What a Lovely War, The Matchgirls* and *Close the Coalhouse Door* show popular songs and music-hall style presentation as an integral part of plays on essentially serious topics. Sometimes the musical elements will dominate. Co-operation with music teachers on the staff could well lead to productions of operas such as Benjamin Britten's *Let's Make an Opera*. Not all music or drama teachers approve of this kind of musical activity, but it can, if approached imaginatively, be genuinely creative.

The rhythms of heart and pulse are at the centre of rhythmic work in movement and music. An understanding of the nature of rhythmic pulse and beat is essential. This can be experienced physically. It can be translated into sound with simple percussive noises which, by subtle combination and arrangement, can produce quite evocative sound sequences for drama work. Variety is found in the degree of vibration ranging from, e.g. the non-vibrating sharp sound of the Chinese block, through vibration such as is heard in a drum to the tremulous quality of the cymbal or gong. Even one instrument is capable of producing a wide variety of sounds varying in percussion and pitch quality. Rhythms based on two, three or four beats can by variation of strength or omission of a beat provide sufficient material for composition for the non-musical teacher. In composition it is important to bear in mind, initially at least, (i) the need for simplicity and a repeated pattern; (ii) making use of the distinctive qualities of the instrument; (iii) contrasts easily gained by a single statement with some embroidery, or an accumulative statement, e.g. A, A + B, A B + C perhaps repeated by a second group of instruments; (iv) increases and decreases of volume and tempo; (v) use of contrasting sound textures. The teacher should not be deterred by a lack of instruments. Home-made drums, shakers and beaters can be quite effective. These sound sequences can be used as simple accompaniments for marching, ceremonial entrances, or to create atmospheric effects of weather, jungle, fairground, outer space and so on.

With the introduction of pitch and melody, the non-specialist may begin to feel out of his depth, but if a musical colleague is consulted concerning the pentatonic scale then a good deal of melodic composition can be attempted. Accompaniments to songs, more sophisticated tunes and additional effects can be composed. The work of Carl Orff makes an important contribution in the area of composition and musical understanding particularly related to percussion. Older pupils might be encouraged to study a scene from a Shakespeare or Chekhov play to find out the range of sound effects that are employed and to devise ways of making those sounds. The sound 'like a harp string breaking' from *The Cherry Orchard* is a famous example. The sound sequences that have been composed by a group of children may be used to accompany existing action or provide a starting point for exploration in movement, mime or dance.

In using existing music, the task becomes much more complex. The temptation is to use music as a substitute for action and emotional sensitivity. Film score music provides both an example and a warning. It can be subtle and evocative or overpowering and sentimental. Music may be used for movement, dance, mime, improvisation or as part of a scripted play. There must be rigorous selection and this entails a considerable amount of listening by the teacher. A collection or library of records and record references must be made. Sets of records for work in movement and mime have been specially devised but they will not always meet the needs of a particular class and sometimes the music is stylistically unattractive. For beginners, short pieces or short extracts from longer compositions should be used. The rhythmic and overall shape should invite a movement dance or dramatic response. So often music is used that is too complex and intricate and leaves the mover baffled and frustrated. No sooner has he attempted to respond to one rhythm or pattern than the music moves forward to a new phrase or development. For these reasons simple pieces with a repetitive rhythm and pattern, a clearly perceived dynamic and of a contained shape are best. As expertise and responsiveness develops, so more sophisticated pieces may be used. Sometimes the music will suggest a step pattern, at others, a shape in the air or response in mime. It might provide the general shape for an improvisation without the specific use of the rhythmic pattern. Dance compositions might make use of more lyrical musical patterns whilst dramatic ideas are likely to relate to changes of tempo, a pause, the climax and contrast of sounds. Some purists will object to music being used in this way and of course some discernment must be applied. It is worth looking at the range of music that ballet and dance companies employ for their choreography to see that a narrowly exclusive view is out of place.

Plays will occasionally call for a formal dance such as a pavane, galliard or waltz. The brilliant tango scene in *Ring Round the Moon* combines and matches the rhythms of speech and dance. Knowledge of some of the basic steps will be useful to the teacher together with some recordings of dance tunes. Seldom can the dances be performed as originally intended because of limitations of space and skill, but a satisfactory effect can be obtained if the music and the steps are danced with confidence and style.

Since several schools of thought exist concerning the relationship of music to movement and drama, the approaches discussed in various books will differ considerably in emphasis. One group sees movement as contributing to musical education, whilst others will see music as the accompaniment of movement work. A third group uses music in a more directly dramatic way, either for mime, improvisation or dramatisation. For all teachers interested in sound and music, John Paynter's *Sound and Silence* provides fascinating reading. Vera Gray and Rachel Percival's *Music, Movement and Mime for Children* discusses the combination of the different elements. Violet Bruce's *Movement in Silence and Sound* is concerned particularly with movement and dance. Some teachers might be interested in Margaret Morris's *My Life in Movement* and the relationship of her work to Carl Orff. Some helpful hints are to be found in Lyn Oxenford's *Playing Period Plays*. Most books on teaching drama include appendices of suitable music for drama with details of recordings (e.g. Brenda Walker's *Teaching Creative Drama*). The BBC pamphlets associated with 'Movement, Mime and Music' and 'Drama Workshop' include extensive lists both of commercial recordings and certain BBC publications. A number of records specially for movement and dance do exist but the teacher will need to listen to them before deciding on their use. Some, whilst suggesting exciting possibilities, prove in the event to be rather disappointing.

7

Radio and Television

It is a great temptation for the over-worked teacher to leaf through the *Radio Times* or *TV Times* and find, with some relief, a schools broadcast that will coincide with his class time-table, to sit back with a sigh to enjoy a respite for twenty minutes or so while the radio or television takes over. One has also seen certain time-tables that seem to be built around schools broadcasts, the teacher having acquired a professional adeptness in switch-flicking and knob-turning. The quality of broadcasts must not be undervalued. They can make a vital contribution to work in a school, particularly in English and drama where the activities demand a good deal of preparation by the teacher and a constant search for fresh material. Used wisely, the broadcast will complement the teacher's own work by adding richness and variety and making possible experiences that the teacher on his own could not provide.

It is obvious that by introducing radio and television into his classroom, the teacher is making a fundamental change in his own role. He is allowing a third party to become involved in the class work, a party over which he has little control, but who can be abruptly removed by the flick of a switch. One would be very chary of inviting a stranger into the classroom to address the pupils without first making some check on his credentials and preparing the children for the visit. At least the same attention must be given before introducing a series of broadcasts. The preparation begins, of course, when the broadcasting companies announce their forthcoming programmes. This they do in good time and in some detail. It is then that the teacher will decide whether a programme has any relevance to the work that he might be doing and to the age of the children that he is teaching. The proposals may work in two ways. Either they are quickly recognised as appropriate to a particular scheme or, equally, they might suggest topics from which the teacher could develop his own individual scheme, i.e. the programmes may complement or initiate ideas for teaching. What they cannot be is specific to one classroom or the individuals in that class. The nature of the medium is such as to make this impossible. Despite all the care that goes into programme planning and pilot schemes, each transmission is to some extent a shot in the dark. However similar to teaching the broadcast appears to be, it is clearly of a different order from the teacher's direct and immediate contact with his class where he is aware and responsive to the particular moment and mood. The programme proceeds – there is little time for questions or interruptions. Uncertainties and ambiguities must be dealt with when the programme is ended or by interrupting it if a tape recording is being used. This means not only is the *teacher's* role changed, but so is the children's, since they have to learn to respond to a different teaching technique. This difference is being stressed because the nature of work in drama is largely dependent upon the pupil/ teacher relationship and the immediacy of the responses that allow the lesson to develop. Thus any teacher contemplating any English or drama programmes must first of all familiarise himself with the content of the broadcast and the method of procedure. Then he can decide the implications so far as his own class is concerned. Needless to say the technical problems related to receivers, tuning, quality of reception must be settled so that no unnecessary interruptions or failures occur. The BBC publish a useful pamphlet, *Using Radio and Television: A Guide to Classroom Practice.* Also the time-tabling of the programmes must be worked out in advance. Some programmes are weekly whilst others are fortnightly. It is permissible to tape the broadcasts so that they may be used at a more convenient time but this still demands adequate equipment and opportunity for the re-cording process.

Still at a practical level, the teacher must see what is actually required for the broadcast. The room must be suitable, e.g. if the notes suggest a hall or large cleared space as the venue, it is unlikely that the programme will be successful in a desk-filled classroom. There must be a supply of Notes for the teacher and an adequate supply of booklets or pamphlets for the children, the cost of which must be budgeted for. The teacher's Notes are a result of very careful preparation and selection. It is foolish to ignore the advice that these Notes contain. Not only do they indicate the precise aim and content of the series, but they also give very full advice on support-ing work and background information. For example, one set of teacher's Notes for *Drama Workshop* considers the aim of the programmes, the role of the teacher, the best method for handling the broadcast, the space required, the type of clothing the participants should be wearing, the necessary ancillary equipment such as rostra, steps, lighting, full notes on development and follow-up and a detailed note on the musical recordings to be used. As well as this introductory information, there is a detailed analysis of the aims and procedures of each lesson, concluding with a list of useful reference books for the teacher. This kind of thoroughness is evident in the preparation of all the broadcasts and indeed the material might well serve as a model scheme of work that teachers could use without actual reference to the broadcasts or if conditions made it impossible to watch or listen. The programmes display a good deal of lively imagination in their compilation and introduce to the teacher ideas that might not otherwise have come his way. The intended age range is always clearly stated. The teacher's experience of his own class will inform him as to whether a class will be receptive to a programme intended for older or younger children, but the temptation to introduce attractive, though obviously inappropriate, broadcasts must be avoided.

For work in drama, both English and drama broadcasts need to be examined since there is usually a strong dramatic element in all the pro-grammes and the follow-up suggestions frequently include improvisation, or dramatisation. Broadly grouped, the B B C broadcasts fall into the follow-ing categories: programmes that (i) provide a stimulus for imaginative response in either speech or writing or both, such as *Speak* or *Living Language*; (ii) supply a rich and varied diet of good quality literary material in the form of poems, jingles, fairy-tales, book extracts (these aim at extending the range of literature with which the children come into contact and a notable feature is the inclusion of specially commissioned work and authors who would not immediately be associated with school broadcast-ing); (iii) invite direct and active participation such as *Drama Workshop* or *Movement, Mime and Music*; (iv) investigate drama as an art form and as a means of communication such as *Drama* and *Scene*.

The dramatic element can be seen to be either as activity arising from a programme that was not specifically drama or one that invites direct involvement with the follow-up either dramatic or extended to relate to other activities in art, music, geography, etc. In each case the teacher's task will be somewhat different. For example, in one series of *Living Language* aimed at children between nine and eleven, a group of broadcasts traces some of Gulliver's travels in Lilliput, Brobdingnag and amongst the Houyhnhnms. An immense variety of activities are suggested to follow the broadcasts including story telling, collecting pictures, reading, discussion, painting. These will involve the provision of books, paper, paint glue, etc.

Also included is 'Act the wise men examining Gulliver, or Gulliver's performance to the crowd, or his encounter with a large animal'. It is important to recognise that this suggestion is significantly different from all the others which allow individual and varying responses. The invitation to act, however, assumes a familiarity with the idea of classroom improvisa-tion and the ability of the children to translate the narrative into drama. This is perfectly possible with a class already acquainted with such pro-cedures, but it will cause unnecessary difficulties if dramatic work is expected to happen without specific preparation. A teacher would not ask the class to paint without making some provision for painting, neither should he, although the demands are minimal, fail to prepare for a dramatic response. A space of some kind is necessary, even if only the corner of the classroom must be reserved. Copies of the pamphlet or any appropriate text written in a style the children can manage must be to hand as well as the improvisation and property box if one exists. Some guidance might be necessary in selecting the scene and shaping it. Careful preparation will allow such an experience to come to a successful conclusion. An art lesson will usually end in a piece of work accomplished. In drama the pupils will often just have reached a point where they are ready to begin. The amount of time needed in drama for an idea to be understood, explored and experienced is usually longer than one would expect. It is frustrating continually to have dramatic work incomplete or postponed, but worst of all completely avoided, because of this time element. The teacher must make clear to the children what activity they are supposed to be engaged in and make provision for the work to get speedily underway. This is most readily done by a careful examination of the pamphlet and the teacher's Notes and by considering how a particular class is likely to respond and plan accordingly. The scale of time in drama is quite different from that in other activities. A piece of writing or a painting can be displayed for a few days without actually absorbing a great deal of time, but drama does not permit this kind of presentation. It literally takes time and provision must be made if the result of the follow-up work is to be shared with the rest of the class. Initially it might be worth allowing a smallish group to develop work in dramatisation and ask the rest of the class to work at different activities.

In a programme such as *Drama Workshop*, the format is much more firmly established. The activity is clearly participatory. The material will already have been conceived in a dramatic form and the actual broadcast itself gives direct stimulus and invites immediate responses in terms of movement, mime or improvisation. The suggestions will encourage an imaginative extension of movement ideas into drama. The teacher will already have received suggestions concerning equipment, music, lighting and projection of slides, etc. The lesson content is usually rich enough to allow further experiment and exploration using the same kinds of stimuli as those used in the broadcast. This is particularly the case with a programme such as *Movement, Mime and Music* where the carefully selected suggestions provide a completely adequate stimulus for further activities. The teacher's Notes include extensive lists of suitable music.

The teacher's role in this kind of broadcast will be very important. He will need to create a sense of involvement by his own personal attitude in, for example, his own dress and occasional participation. He will need to *observe* the children's responses to particular parts of the broadcast and decide what further activities are possible. He will see where lively ideas invite further development, where a stimulus is incompletely absorbed and needs reinforcement perhaps by a suggestion from the children's own experience. In a group of broadcasts on the elements, Earth, Air, Fire and

Water, for example, local anecdotes related to a fire, the launching of a new aircraft, or a sea rescue might receive mention. Opportunities to extend into forms of activity other than dramatic should not be omitted. The broadcaster in *Movement, Mime and Music Stage 2* expresses the hope in his notes that the follow-up will help to integrate English, geography, maths, history and all other 'subjects'. This programme, whilst emphasising music and movement stimuli also includes visual and literary material and should not be thought of as pursuing a very specialist concept in either movement, mime or music, each of which, in other circumstances, could be considered a distinct discipline. It is a feature of all the programmes that they draw on a rich range of sources including stories, poems, pictures, music.

In the secondary programmes *Books, Plays, Poems* and *Speak*, aimed at both fostering creative appreciation and stimulating talk, a more precise differentiation is made between dramatisation and dramatic texts that actually start life as plays. The programmes invite responses in terms of speech, in comment, discussion and improvised drama. Some kind of distinction should be possible between these various activities. It is important not to allow the responses to become an undifferentiated stream of speech/comment/improvisation. The TV programme *Drama* shows drama very much more as an art form. Actual plays or scenes are performed, but the selection is for thematic rather than theatrical reasons. With the introduction of the visual element, the dramatic impact is considerably intensified. Physical characteristics and environment are more clearly defined. It can be argued that the nature of the imaginative response changes. No longer are the figures and the landscape in the unseen, free ranging world of sound, but limited in time and place. This may or may not be an advantage. (Certain radio programmes also have visual accompaniments. They are known as Radiovision.)

The thematic approach can be illustrated by a recent series described as a comment on 'human beings generally and the way they behave'. This rather loose title comes into a sharper focus when you see that the plays selected are *Chips with Everything, Hobson's Choice*, and *A Taste of Honey*. This selection immediately suggests classroom work either in further examination of the plays presented or a search for other plays that contribute to the same theme. Many plays that might otherwise remain vague or incompletely understood become meaningful to pupils through such introductions and comparisons.

The IBA also offers a substantial number of programmes for schools. There is a tendency for the work in English and drama to be approached through programmes grouped round a particular topic. Often the theme has an immediate relevance to activities in other lessons such as art or social studies. The broadcast functions as an integrating unit and will be particularly valuable in schools where there are less rigid time-table divisions. It is very important to recognise this thematic approach and plan for it. The future programmes are announced well ahead and there is plenty of information available to the teacher in the Annual Programme booklet, the newspaper *ITV Education* and, of course in the programme literature. *Picture Box* for the 8–11 age group supplies stimulating visual material to which a response can be made in writing, art or movement. Items from one series include the Bayeux Tapestry, a Czech puppet fantasy, cave paintings and steam locomotives. A programme such as *Fusion*, as the title implies explores drama, music, poetry, art, sculpture and moves freely from one form to another. Here it is essential that the teacher is fully prepared so that ideas suggested can be followed up. The scope is very wide. *Rules, Rules, Rules* examines the situations of the young in society whilst *Drama* and *Conflict* use more specifically dramatic material. Plays in one *Conflict* series include such varied titles as *The Duchess of Malfi, Richard II, The School for Scandal* and *Hobson's Choice*. Another programme, *The Messengers,* presents authors, playwrights and poets discussing their approach to writing.

Both the BBC and IBA have Education Officers in the various regions of the country who visit schools and test the effectiveness of the broadcasts and gather or distribute information. Both channels invite children's contributions and these are often used in subsequent broadcasts. This is a valuable activity both in itself and as a demonstration of a real contact with the broadcasters who are heard either as disembodied voices issuing from a loudspeaker or as shadows in a television tube.

It will be noted that no critical appraisal has been offered of the programmes. This can only be done effectively by the teacher who must be sensitive in his own responses, and willing to discuss the broadcasts with his colleagues and the children. Rigour in selection is vital and the teacher should be ready to discontinue a broadcast when it is clearly ceasing to be of any value to his particular class.

Of course many programmes of educational interest occur outside Schools broadcasts. There is plenty of evidence that children are among the most avid watchers of television. There is scope for a great deal of discussion and comment on evening and weekend programmes. Too much watching can have disadvantages other than the health ones so far as drama is concerned. What is at first considered to be a lively and imaginative invention is later recognised as an imitation of an incident from a popular series. The teacher should be in a position to realise this and avoid suggestions that connect too directly with current programmes, unless of course a reference is particularly valuable as a basis for further exploration. For example, a *Movement, Mime and Music* series includes a theme, *Space 2000*. Obviously any reference to space travel or rocket launching will be invaluable and the children should be invited to recall and re-create what they had seen on the screen. The teacher should be quick to take advantage of any broadcast that will clarify, enrich or enlighten any work that he is doing.

It will have become clear that far from being an easy option, the use of radio and television broadcasts requires a good deal of expertise on the part of the teacher. He must become adept in the technical aspects of tuning and controlling the sound and vision. He will need to know the techniques for making tape recordings from broadcasts. He will have to plan his time-table to avoid interruption while the programmes are in progress and ensure that the supporting material such as pamphlets, charts, slides, etc., are available. He will need to respond quickly to the material being broadcast so that the follow-up work can proceed without too much delay. He will have to estimate what activities are likely to develop. He will want his class to participate actively in the broadcasts so that any requests for children's writing, poems, illustration, etc., will provoke contributions from his class.

If these conditions can be met, the teacher will find that using the BBC and IBA broadcasts will provide him with a valuable approach to drama. The programmes are very carefully prepared and the broadcasters have immense resources on which they can draw. But co-operation and involvement by the teacher is vital if the work is to have any creative value as drama.

Both the IBA and BBC publish annual programmes that describe future plans in detail. They include the time-table of broadcasts and notes of preview and repeat dates. Also listed are addresses of Education Officers and publications. The BBC's *Using Radio and Television: A Guide to Classroom Practice* and *School Radio and the Tape Recorder* give guidance on classroom procedure and the efficient use of tape recordings. The pamphlets for the actual broadcasts are also a good source of material and suggestions.

Discussion of closed circuit television has been omitted from this survey because of the technical requirements, but Roderick McLean's *Television in Education* provides a helpful introduction for those teachers who have the opportunity to develop this work.

8

Drama and Related Subjects

Many will be familiar with the famous tableaux in Madame Tussaud's depicting the death of Nelson, the execution of Mary Queen of Scots or other famous and infamous historical events. The presenters recognise that by creating a feeling of actuality, by offering representations of the historical figures at a particular place and moment a vivid sense of the occasion is evoked, more immediate than that contained in a printed description in book or document. Dramatists have been quick to seize on historic events or personages to supply the subject matter of their plays though the results have not always had historical validity. The Greek dramatist Aeschylus reprimanded by a critic for causing the wrong side to win in his dramatic version of a famous battle (historically the opponents were victors) replied that it was not the job of the dramatist to write history. Very much more recently, quite vigorous debate was conducted concerning Rolf Hochhuth's *Soldiers* which was considered to attribute to Winston Churchill actions and attitudes that had no basis in fact. It would be naïve to accept as historically accurate Shakespeare's view of the Wars of the Roses. His unflattering portrait of Richard III has caused many historians to protest at the distortion. It is seldom the dramatist's intention to write straightforward history, rather does he see the particular events and people incorporate an idea or concept which he wishes to explore and shape in dramatic terms. He quite readily adjusts the order of events and the characteristics of the participants to conform to his central ideas. Inevitably there is a reduction in the detail of the actual historical record, a careful selection from the usually over-abundant material, and a framework constructed, which though historically inaccurate finally gives the play a cogent, dramatic shape.

Although there is a clear difference of aim between the historian and the dramatist, it is not to say there is no place for drama or dramatic methods in history or geography. A television commentator reporting on the horticulture industry in California where there was alleged exploitation of Mexican fieldworkers, continually referred to Steinbeck's novel *The Grapes of Wrath*. Comparisons between the novel and the contemporary situation were very vivid. Economics and processes of horticulture, picketing, arguments between owner, union official, worker and housewife held equally important places in the novel and the reported situation. This example may provide a key to one of the connections between drama and subjects such as geography and history. Although the novel (it could equally have been a play) offered a simplified, carefully organised, literary representation of a particular conflict, it still identified the major problem and the accompanying human predicament. Shaw's *St Joan* and Arthur Miller's *The Crucible* are very famous plays derived from historical events, but neither offers a precise reconstruction. A new type of play has been developed recently that makes use of very precise transcripts of real events, e.g. *The Oz Trial*, but that play still remains very distinct from the actual proceedings. Rather do they represent honest attempts to identify the fundamental issues and reveal them in dramatic terms of character and plot. Drama is just as much a process of seeking the truth as distorting it and the dramatic approach can serve a very valuable purpose in exploring and identifying issues and attitudes of the personalities that are intimately concerned.

If such exploration takes place in the classroom then certain requirements must be observed. A great deal of what passes for historical dramatisation would be more aptly described as 'charades'. First, the historical or geographical material must be dramatically viable. It must be of such a shape that allows exposition in conversation and action rather than long-winded narration. The chief personalities must have some inherent attractiveness. The focus should preferably be concentrated on one or two important events, rather than encompassing a whole story in a string of brief underdeveloped sequences. The telescoping of time, the rearrangements of events, the invention of additional characters – all are permissible. Much historical material is very intransigent and dramatic treatment should be accorded only to events that have some obviously dramatic appeal – a conflict and its resolution, a search and discovery, events containing contrasting individuals or groups, the progress of an outstanding character, a letter or document containing news of great change or importance. These are the types of situations that invite dramatisation. Actual historical documents, or replicas (the Jackdaw packs contain good samples) items of clothing, eyewitness reports or other primary sources can provide useful starting points. Dramatic exploration brings events under close scrutiny. Characters must be firmly portrayed. Where the historical document or commentary overlooks or omits, the detail must be imagined or invented. The search for motivation may well start all kinds of inquiries that otherwise are conveniently ignored. The improvising actors have to align themselves with particular characters and imaginatively extend their personalities from the profile presented in the historical documents. This can be a revealing process. One is forced to identify the motives and attitudes in a very personal way. Whilst John Osborne's *Luther* is in no sense a historical documentary, it nevertheless gives valuable insights into the problems of the period and Luther's personal difficulties from a number of differing viewpoints. Similarly, the improvisations or even written sequences for acting relating to a particular moment of decision or argument may well help to clarify the issue in human terms. A characteristic of drama is that it demands commitment. The historian may write an account leaving certain questions unanswered, the author can justifiably comment on the uncertainty of the evidence and offer alternative accounts. Dramatically, decisions must be made and the search for the precise and real truth becomes more insistent. The alternatives can be worked out in practical terms and relative probabilities compared. Perhaps through dramatic exploration can arise the realisation of the extreme difficulty in arriving at a precise and accurate description of an historic event and the recognition of how much is conjectural in what purports to be an accurate unbiased report.

Margaret S. Anderson's *Splendour of Earth* is an anthology of descriptive physical geography. The excerpts illustrate the strangeness, wonder and strength of the forces of nature as they are recorded, not by expert geographers, but by writers of contemporary literature. The descriptions of deserts, earthquakes and glaciers are as varied as are the authors, Robert Bridges, Joseph Conrad, T. S. Eliot, Evelyn Waugh. Miss Anderson, in making her choices, used three criteria. She chose accounts that would stimulate the imagination more than would the ordinary textbook; recognisable descriptions of real physical features in real places; extracts that were both accurate and vivid. Miss Anderson's method of selection and choice show what a contribution literature can make to other subjects. No dramatic extracts are included, but it would be perfectly possible to construct a companion volume that includes plays whose very fabric and dramatic intensity lies in the precise geographical location of the action, as it affects the characters and their life style. At one level of creativity it can be said that Shakespeare's *The Tempest* had its genesis in the famous 'Bemoothes' pamphlets which described the discovery of a paradisal island in the Western Atlantic. At a more prosaic level, Arnold Wesker's *Roots* captures the life style of an isolated Norfolk village and the particular tensions it creates in matters of employment, farming and communication in a rural community. O'Neill's *Desire Under the Elms*, Williams's *Night of the Iguana*, Kirkland's *Tobacco Road* are a powerful group of American plays that depend considerably upon the particular locations in which characters react violently to the pressures created by environment. O'Neill's earthy New England landscape with the dazzling prospect of California dangled as a bait; the debilitating damp heat of the Mexican climate; the rural squalor of *Tobacco Road*: all the settings contribute vitally to the plays. It is obvious that such references will play a relatively small part in any geography scheme, and it is not suggested that there is such an educational process as 'geography through drama', but the possibility, at least, of reference to dramatic material should not be entirely rejected.

In the classroom situation, as with the historic material, geography can offer centres of attention around which episodes can be improvised or dramatised. It is not insignificant that in school broadcasting, dramatisation plays a very large part because it is recognised as a means of giving a lively and imaginative approach to teaching geography. Certain pitfalls must be avoided however. Perhaps geography as opposed to history is less dependent upon a particular person at a particular time. It is more concerned with processes and wide-scale events that might not have a specifically human reference. Whilst it might be tempting to begin a dramatic project on 'A Day in the Life of . . .', the result (though it may be geographically informative) is not necessarily going to be dramatically effective. It is preferable to centre the work on some particular event or moment where a great change is occuring or where some feature evokes responses in dramatic terms. In the Museum of the Planetarium in Vancouver, a section is devoted to the geography of the Rockies supported by a large number of exhibits related to timber, fishing, the Gold Rush, etc. This last stand is particularly rich in dramatic ideas. Indeed it is astonishing to see how many songs, adventure stories and plays have emerged from that period. It certainly invites a dramatic response. The maps, charts, diaries, letters, equipment lists, warrants and charters as well as the actual items of equipment and photographs of leading figures and accounts of their exploits all offer starting points. The teacher should ensure that the work undertaken should gather a dramatic rather than descriptive impetus. It will undoubtedly encourage close investigation and observation and can succeed in transmitting to the children a vivid sense of a particular place and its people.

Perhaps dramatisation in history and geography is most useful as a contribution to a project where ideas are being presented in a variety of ways with displays, exhibitions, charts, models and dramatisations. The existence of so many dull, tediously drawn out and patently undramatic historical pageants should serve as a dire warning against length and prolixity. The actual procedures for improvisation and play-making in the classroom are given detailed discussion in other chapters.

'GAMES' AND ROLE PLAY

Rex Walford in *Games in Geography* describes a geography project in the shape of a game connected with the development of the railway systems of the USA in the nineteenth century. The class divides into teams each of which forms a company board. The members are elected to play the roles of treasurer, surveyor, detective, secretary, chairman, etc., each having specific duties. The companies are faced with the task of building a railway system and overcoming a series of financial, territorial and climatic problems as well as the competition from rival concerns. The rules of play vary in difficulty and complexity according to the age of the class concerned. Regular board meetings are held on the issues as they occur, particularly since 'Chance' cards can throw up unforeseen difficulties. The aim of the exercise is to introduce the general problems of railway building, developing an understanding of the geography and history of the USA and encouraging co-operation in discussion and decision making. Now this game might seem to have only vague connections with drama and the purist might well raise horrified objections. It may also seem some distance from geography as critics have already suggested. It does however contain some basic features of drama. Clearly there is role play. The team members have to act 'as if' they were chairman, secretary, etc. A chapter in Mr Walford's book describing a classroom experience of his game notes some very vivid characterisation. There is an objective to be achieved, but only by overcoming difficulties (again a basic dramatic situation) and the whole activity takes place within a structure where all the class observe certain mutually accepted conventions. There are also features in common with improvisation and play-making techniques used by the professional theatre companies in their school visits when social or political problems are tackled in a similar way by providing certain information and planning meetings, discussions and demonstrations through a dramatic role-playing approach.

Problem solving through role play has certainly gained impetus during the past few years in management training. A recent television programme showed a 'game' being played at an Oxford college with individuals (not actors) in the roles of various Government ministers, Officials and Service chiefs in conflict over a contemporary political issue. Theories were tested, conferences held, documentation was provided and ideas argued out by the various factions. The 'game' projected a real political problem and the participants were required to respond imaginatively in their adopted roles. The result was deeply revealing as the final discussion of the whole situation disclosed. The methods were clearly related to drama. Perhaps it could best be described as a sophisticated, intellectualised development of dramatic play.

The words 'game' and 'role playing' need, perhaps, a little more discussion at this juncture. N. V. Scarfe in an address delivered to the Geographical Association (*Geography*, July 1971) devoted his time to considering the place of games in geography teaching. He referred to an article by Ingar and Stoll, 'Games as Learning' (*Journal of Educational Studies*, 1970) listing the characteristics of games as: activities freely engaged in; their purpose, uniquely pleasure and fun; in essence, unproductive; challenges to a task or opponent; symbolic activities governed by rules; arbitrary, limited and separated in time and space from real life activities. On the other hand Rex Walford reminds us (*Games in Geography*) of Marshall McLuhan's view that 'Games, like art, are a translator of experience'. Perhaps the truth lies somewhere between these two attitudes. The game, whether boxing or Monopoly, has, like the play, a formalised or stylised structure and undoubtedly employs or invites symbolic interpretations. Within the form, however, a very lifelike situation is developed. Real-life crises are explored, real confrontation or competition takes place. There is a simulation of reality. Real life experience and actual 'know-how' will be invaluable. In some 'simulation' exercises the 'real-life' element is almost 100 per cent, though there is always a recognition that the activity can be terminated. The game makes use of actual experience and can also supply first-hand experience in situations that might otherwise remain closed for the participants. It provides and uses experience. Perhaps in directly commercial terms it is unproductive, yet it can produce stimulating ideas and be both educative and informative in the process.

The term 'role play' has been very thoroughly explained by psychologists and educationalists in very complex psychological terms. The degree of consciousness on the part of the individual concerned is significant. Assuming a reasonable degree of consciousness, the person takes the role of someone other than himself and by his own observation, sensitivity and personal responses attempts to re-create that other person and to respond as he would in the situations that confront him. The activity may take place at an imitative level or in the case of an actor as a result of long training and experience. The actor's investigation will combine practical, aesthetic and intellectual aspects. He is often called upon to create roles very far removed from everyday normal reality. Whilst remaining himself he has to respond 'as if' he were someone else with different physical characteristics, attitudes and thoughts. He draws upon his own experiences, the play text and the responses of his fellow actors (all engaged on similar tasks) and suggestions that arise from discussion with the director. This is, of course, a very refined, sophisticated type of role play. In the rather looser form of 'game' activities, the role play will not be so formally and strongly governed, but many of the other characteristics will remain. The 'as if' element remains prominent and the need to respond in terms distinct from one's own very personal views is vitally important. Also necessary is the ability to sustain that attitude through a series of planned and free ranging activities. It must be recognised that this is a fairly demanding task and the difficulties appreciated.

If these two rather simple descriptions of 'game' and 'role play' can be accepted, it is possible to recognise a set of conditions that will make the activities in which they are employed more likely to be successful. The game in geography has been referred to only as a convenient example. There are a whole host of activities that could lend themselves to exploration in terms of games, role playing or simulations of real situations: mock debates, parliaments, trials, interviews, speeches, explorations in schemes such as the Nuffield Humanities Project and ventures in theatre education such as those carried out by the Belgrade Company. First there must be the recognition that although a game is being played or a situation simulated, it is to be serious and in as 'real-life' terms as possible. A general framework must be created that shows the limits within which the participants must operate. The materials for investigation must be as realistic as possible. For example, in a mock interview discussing a job vacancy, there should be a precise job specification with information about training, etc., rather than a vaguely defined job existing 'somewhere'. In a project on local government, the actual organisation, representatives and officials of a particular area must be identified. The 'Toy Town' image is to be avoided. As in the geography game when realistic maps and statistics were provided, so any project requiring documentation should have the appropriate material available. In a mock Parliament, copies of Hansard, newspaper accounts and radio reports should be studied. Information concerning the organisation of the House of Commons and at least some of the procedures for debate should be available. In exploratory projects, field trips, library visits should be included. The Nuffield Humanities Project on 'War and Society' contains an excellent range of extracts from diaries, books, reports, newspapers and photographs, posters and films, all of which give realistic support to the investigation.

It is almost impossible to specify precise procedure, but if the pattern of the actual activity being studied can be adopted, then a reasonable working plan may emerge. For instance in the case of an interview, the documentation, advertisement, application form, etc., should be carefully studied before the interview takes place and not produced as an afterthought. An actual council session might suggest a model to adopt. Even if the conditions demand a simplification of the proceedings they should, nevertheless, have some kind of order and relevance to the actual. Every attempt must be made to supply real or realistic evidence and documentation. The outstanding problem is undoubtedly the one of simplification, the containing of an immensely complex idea within the confines of the game. It is in the area of selection that a scheme will be most tested. For example in any study of local goverment the tangle of laws and relationships between central, regional and local authorites combine to thwart any true presentation in simple terms. Often TV programmes have attempted to investigate a local issue and the only result is recrimination and anger. The teacher should try to ensure that some useful study is achieved even when it becomes obvious that no solution is possible.

Perhaps some dramatic models may be helpful both to the teacher in showing how a pattern can be developed and the pupils in understanding the roles they are to play and the locations in which they find themselves placed. Playwrights have always had to face this problem of simplification and containment. The Biblical story of Solomon's judgement concerning the two women claiming the same baby may be compared with Brecht's version of a similar claim in *The Caucasian Chalk Circle*. *Inherit the Wind* provides a fascinating trial scene, as does *The Caine Mutiny Court Martial* or, in a lighter vein, the trial of Mr Pickwick. *St Joan* and *The Merchant of Venice* make interesting examples of ecclesiastical and legal proceedings and there is a forceful cross-examination in *The Winslow Boy*. All these episodes require the setting to be clearly suggested and the characters, judge, jury, inquisitors identified. But whereas the actor/pupil will derive his character from a study of the play and a recognition of the total dramatic pattern, the role-playing judge is required to improvise not from his own personal and private viewpoint but from that of the character he is impersonating. It follows therefore that the pupil must have some means of acquainting himself with the demands of the role and it is to be expected that his first efforts at vocalisation are likely to be tentative and unsustained. Any previous dramatic experience will be valuable at this point. First attempts at role play and simulation should be brief and fairly simple. With experience, more complex topics and more extended and sustained role play become possible. It will be helpful if pupils make private dossiers on themselves in their roles, adding information and comments on attitudes as they are revealed. The great danger in role play is for it to remain superficial and basically unserious.

The main objective in the work is investigatory, carried out not from a distant academic viewpoint, but with active involvement and commitment. Whilst acutely aware of his own feelings, the participant is required to examine the motives and consciousness of others. Emotion, prejudice and intellect vie for supremacy. It is possible that subsequently the pupil's own judgement may become more sober, rational and informed.

This kind of activity might have a place in geography, history, social studies, documentary drama and improvisation. It could supplement specific work in drama or create drama in its own terms.

DOCUMENTARY DRAMA

The Times (23 April 1971) reported that the secretary of a local Labour Party, attempting to publicise a forthcoming municipal election, was supplementing the traditional canvassing with a street morality play. The central figure was to be 'John Small', the villain, the Conservative Party, 'Feed-the-Rich', and the Labour Party 'Care-for-man'. The play explored the local situation and characters, and by applying the rules of Cockney slang, the personalities could be readily identified. The people were being urged to exercise their voting rights. It may be that the material collected from a particular project could be used for play-making in a variety of styles. Certainly professional playwrights have not hesitated to make use of political or social issues to produce documentary style. Examples are found in plays such as *Cathy Come Home* or Joan Littlewood's production of *The Protector*, which was undoubtedly influenced by the disaster at Ronan Point where, after an explosion, a section of the building collapsed. *Oh What a Lovely War* despite its boisterous and seaside Poirot style of performance made a pointed and poignant comment on the destructiveness of the First World War.

What might emerge from exploration or examination of a social or political topic is some form of documentary drama. This is not an easy form to manipulate. The rules for constructing the well-made play do not apply. It is likely to be episodic in structure, but some endeavour should be made to maintain a strong unifying line in the shape of a particular character or a carefully constructed time scale. Each episode should concentrate on making a single main point and then juxtaposed with contrasting scenes, songs or sketches that comment or amplify. The concert device of *Oh What a Lovely War* was a brilliant invention and it should not be assumed that all documentary drama need be in a directly realistic style. There is plenty of room for inventiveness and diversity, but it should not become shapeless.

To summarise the approaches described so far, they may be classified as follows:

(1) The use of literary or dramatic examples that identify, albeit in theatrical terms, hstorical, socio.ogical or political issues within the form of a play. These texts can never be considered as 'pure' history or politics since the framatisation inevitably demands reduction in scale, and complexity, but they remain valuable in their imaginative presentation of an issue which may provoke discussion or invite further exploration. Often in a complicated issue it is impossible to see the wood for the trees. Plays or play extracts may provide appropriate 'copses' where both 'tree' and 'wood' are sufficiently isolated for thoughtful observation.

(2) Materials in history, geography, etc., may be investigated by improvisation or play-making techniques in order to re-create the actuality of the moment or identify the real issue. The method attempts to evoke and transmit the human responses involved. It makes demands upon the imagination, it requires conjecture and deduction and it illustrates the difficulty of establishing the real facts.

(3) At a second level, the investigation requires a deeper sense of engagement. The participants become more seriously involved, either in terms of a game supported with realistic equipment where the problem solving is the dominant feature, or in the free, role playing situation with individual commitment and the need to explore motives and attitudes and respond to them. Although certain conventions remain, within the pattern there is an attempt to simulate a real life situation. The overall aim is to sharpen sensitivity and increase awareness in matters of judgement, decision making and human attitudes.

(4) Documentary drama draws material from real life and it is often collected from a particular locality and relates to specific issues. It adopts a dramatic form without adhering to any traditional modes of playwriting or theatrical presentation. The nature of dramatic reality is significantly different from the actual reality so that rigorous selection must therefore take place. Although documentary drama is really operating at the level of communication rather than as an art, theatrical devices such as lighting, staging, costume, film, TV, etc., may be used and acting, singing and dancing included. (Alan Plater's *Close the Coalhouse Door* is a good example.) Some experience in handling the theatrical aspects is likely to help the whole venture to be successfully accomplished.

How should a teacher prepare himself to undertake work in any of the areas outlined above? He must decide as clearly as he can what he hopes the outcome will be. A vaguely held notion of 'something' emerging is not good enough. The expectation need not be rigidly adhered to if, as the project develops, alternative patterns suggest themselves. But the teacher must know if, on the one hand, he is working towards a conclusion or whether, on the other, the concern is solely for the process of discovery and examination. The procedure for creating a documentary drama to be presented to fellow pupils or even to the public is quite different from role play in job finding or examining the political situation in South Africa. In the latter cases the teacher will be expecting his pupils to express and verbalise thoughts and emotions that in the normal classroom situation might remain unspoken. He will be urging involvement and commitment and the atmosphere must encourage confidence and ease. The convention of the game or improvisation must be explained so that the pupils understand the rules of behaviour. It is disastrous to encourage free speech and then abruptly deny it without warning. Reality has a habit of becoming a 'hot potato'.

Where reference is to be made to historical or political events, there must be abundant documentation and supporting evidence. Before the topic is started a thorough search for material must take place. Relevant books, newspaper cuttings, magazine articles, film strips, pictures, statistical data must be to hand. Facts and opinions will be assembled as the work proceeds, but the diverse and contradictory nature of documentary evidence must be understood from the start. Research and assessment of evidence must be encouraged. Visits to libraries, museums, art galleries, etc., will have to be arranged. It is foolish to attempt to simulate reality whilst ignoring real evidence which is close at hand.

The process of sorting and sifting evidence and translating it into dramatic terms is time consuming and complex. There is an assumption of considerable expertise on the part of the teacher and his pupils. It is easy to expect too much. Initially very simple projects should be attempted so that the experience gained can be used later. It might be worth studying dramatic scripts where playwrights have grappled with similar problems or to observe the procedure in radio and television programmes attempting this particular approach.

The teacher should familiarise himself with the techniques of improvisation and playmaking and scripting so that the work is not held up by a lack of preparedness. Discussions with colleagues who have particular expertise will help. They might even volunteer to participate in the work making more lesson time available. The work should be planned in a series of units so that the progress can be built up into some meaningful pattern. There need not necessarily be dramatic development, but a sense of increasing coherence should emerge.

Peter Head and R. Verrier in the Appendixes to *Drama and Theatre in Education* describe projects they undertook, one in connection with the assassination of President Kennedy and the other, a study of the Civil War in England. Their very valuable commentaries show how the projects were shaped by the topic. In the assassination inquiry, the actual play, after preliminary planning, was composed in one day and then performed to an audience who afterwards participated in discussion. The second scheme created the need for considerable research. The war was discussed from a number of viewpoints. Speeches, pamphlets and diaries were composed. Experiments with dramatised tape recordings were undertaken. Mr Verrier was against pre-planning that did not allow for pupils' interests to develop. The preparatory work should be conjectural rather than prescriptive.

Brian Way's *Development Through Drama* contains a helpful chapter on social drama and John Hodgson's *Improvisation* gives information concerning the development of improvisation techniques. Several chapters in Richard Courtney's *Play, Drama and Thought* fill in the background to role theories. Information concerning simulation and games can be found in Rex Walford's *Games in Geography* and *Simulation in the Classroom* (written with J. L. Taylor), Boocock and Schild's *Simulation, Game and Learning* and P. J. Tansey's *Educational Aspects of Simulation.*

It is fairly clear that the teacher will need to make a good deal of personal preparation before undertaking any scheme in this area of approach. It is an important way of introducing subjects that have a real and direct relevance to children's lives and enables them to come to terms with them, not head-on or in abstract terms, but by search, discovery and commitment. Whilst the activity cannot be labelled drama, it utilises the dramatic and may, in fact, lead to work in drama in one form or another.

An Interlude: Acting Shakespeare in your Classroom*

Although Shakespeare wrote his plays (all thirty-seven of them) nearly four hundred years ago, they are still performed today – and performed, probably, more often than ever before, all over the world – because they bring alive particularly good stories: stories that are full of excitement and adventure and interesting characters; stories about things that are always with us or near us in our lives – such things as human foolishness or goodness, feelings of love and hate, courage and fear, ambition, loyalty, the instincts of revenge and forgiveness, the wish to kill and the dreadful consequences of killing. All these things, and many more, we are bound to meet in one form or another in the course of our own lives; and they can all be found alive in one way or another somewhere in Shakespeare's work.

He did more, though, than write a lot of successful plays. He acted in them himself. He helped to run the theatre in which he and his fellow-actors worked. He shared with them all the backstage crafts and tasks that have to go on before any performance can be presented to the public. In other words, Shakespeare, like all the other players in his company, was an all-round, professional man of the theatre, thoroughly trained in all its arts. He wrote his plays for a small group of people – smaller in fact than the size of your class – whom he knew well and was used to working with. Indeed, he seems, sometimes, to have created a character with the gifts of a particular actor specially strongly in his mind. And this point brings up the first and most important thing to remember when you come to look at a piece of his text for the first time. *Shakespeare wrote his plays to be acted, not just to be read.* The next was first and foremost a *script* for a team of actors and technicians to work from; it showed them what to say and what to *do* in order to make a performance; it was something to be turned into *action* by a group of people, not something to be merely read to themselves in stillness and quiet.

Shakespeare's theatre was different from ours in many ways. For one

---

* This article, by Christopher Parry, is from Fowler and Dick's *English 11/12* (Allen & Unwin, 1971).

thing it was much smaller; for another it was an open air place. If you have never seen a drawing or a painting of The Globe, or any other typical Elizabethan theatre, try to find one, or ask your teacher to find one. It was a roughly circular building and the stage jutted out into the middle of the circle. This was the main acting area, with a light roof over most of it, supported by two large pillars at the front. Many of the audience – those who paid the cheapest prices for their places stood on the ground, in the open, round the three sides of the stage, to watch the play: richer folk sat in the narrow, covered galleries situated in three tiers round the sides of the building. There were doors at each side of the main stage at the back, through which the characters entered and left the scene. Between the doors there was a small inner room which could be hidden from view by curtains across the front. Above this room was a balcony, used when an upper scene was needed (as for the famous love scene between Romeo and Juliet); and above this again there was a tiny gallery where the company's musicians sometimes played their instruments, when music was required. There was no curtain across the front of the main stage. There was no artificial light, so plays were performed much earlier than is usual nowadays, before dusk fell. There was no scenery, apart from furniture like thrones, tables, stools and so on, and items that the actors could carry with them, like flags and banners, swords and goblets. The actors wore splendid costumes, usually in the Elizabethan style of Shakespeare's day, whatever period the story of the play belonged to. And the whole playhouse was very much smaller than a modern theatre: from front to back it was probably no more than two or three times the length of your classroom: so the actors and the audience were much closer together than they are today.

This meant, among other things, that people could hear the words of the play clearly and easily – and audiences in those days were used to *listening* to a play, as they watched it, more carefully than most audiences listen nowadays. Similarly, actors spoke their lines a good deal more carefully than many actors do today. For the words of the play were *vital*. Through them Shakespeare stirred the imagination of his spectators, rousing them to see with their minds' eye all that he wanted them to see: and through the words that the characters spoke Shakespeare showed his actors all that he wanted them to do. Almost all the stage directions in his text are not Shakespeare's at all; they have been added by people who printed his plays after his death. He told his actors what to do *through the lines themselves*; and he expected them to understand what he was telling them in this way, and to act accordingly. For instance, when Oberon and Titania are drawing near for their first face-to-face encounter of the play (each about to enter through one of the doors on to the main stage) Puck and the Fairy say this:

Puck: But room, fairy! here comes Oberon.
Fairy: And here my mistress. – Would that he were gone!

It is clear from this that Puck and the Fairy see their master and mistress approaching just before the audience do; that Puck tries to hustle the Fairy out of the way before Oberon arrives ('But room, fairy!') that the Fairy won't be hustled right away because her mistress is near by; that the quarrel between Oberon and Titania, which Puck has referred to earlier in the scene, is likely to flare up ('Would that he were gone!'), so that the two servant-fairies draw back anxiously as the royal pair approach. Shakespeare packs all these 'acting instructions' into two short lines. And all the time the words of the play are working hard like this to help the imagination of the actors and the audience. Look, for instance, at the way the opening of this scene (like Titania's call for a lullaby and the song itself, later) suggest the world of nature where it is all taking place and, at the same time, the tiny size of the fairies.

These fairies, incidentally, are quite unlike any others that you will ever read about. Shakespeare created them specially for this play, and there is nothing in the least bit soft or babyish about any of them. Indeed, Oberon and Titania behave just like any pair of proud and angry human grown-ups involved in a petty squabble; and their servants are a thoroughly spry and mischievous lot, with Puck the most cheeky and impish of all – like any set of 11 to 12 year-olds! In fact, these parts were originally acted by boys of about that age (and so were all the *female* characters in the play, for ladies never appeared on the public stage in Shakespeare's time). These boys were often skilful actors already, although so young, because they were training to be adult players in the company later on.

Pupils today are often a little puzzled, when they look at a piece of Shakespeare for the first time, to find that what the characters say is set out, for the most part, in *lines* that look like poetry but don't always rhyme. Shakespeare had a good reason for doing this. If you look carefully at the speeches (not the songs) you will find that most of the lines have ten syllables – occasionally Shakespeare lops one off or adds on an extra one – and most of the lines have five strong beats in them:

The kìng doth keèp his rèvels hère tonìght.

This arrangement, built into the words, made it easier for the actors to learn their parts; and they had to do this quickly sometimes, for they might perform three different plays in one week!

The best way of getting to know what Shakespeare is like is to try to act something he wrote – such as this extract from his comedy *A Midsummer Night's Dream*. Before starting, ask your teacher to tell you or read to you the story of the whole play, so that you can see how this piece fits into the rest and, in particular, how the one *human* character in this extract –

Bottom the Weaver, a simple man, comic like his name – comes to be wandering about in the fairy world, in the strangest of disguises. The next thing you need is a space to act in – which may mean pushing aside some of the desks in your classroom (not a difficult operation, with a bit of care and planning); if you can manage more than one level (for instance, a low platform of some kind, for Titania to sleep on, is useful) so much the better. Apart from something representing Oberon's flower and something else for Bottom's headpiece, you don't *have* to have anything else – the words will do the trick, if you attend to them carefully – but any extras you can manage will all add to the effect. Even the smallest bit of dressing up will help enormously. You don't need to swamp the actors in clothes; just try to find something that will suggest clearly the difference between the royal fairies and the servant fairies, and the difference between the fairies on the one hand and the humans on the other. Music, too, is very helpful in setting the mood for this sequence, and for accompanying the lullaby, – if there is any way of providing it. If it is difficult to find anyone to sing, the lullaby can be spoken quietly, with music played softly behind it; Bottom's song, on the other hand, ought to be loud, vigorous, and quite out of tune.

But, more than anything else, it's the words that matter. You don't have to learn them by heart – in fact, you will be surprised at how quickly you can get used to acting from the book held in one hand – but you *do* need to look out, all the time, for what they are telling you about what the characters are doing, what they are feeling, how they are moving, when they come and go, how they react, and so on. If you have a part to act, it's best to read through it carefully beforehand, and in the performance not to try to read it too fast. To get the best out of the script Shakespeare's actors never gabbled. If you find some of the words in the script difficult to say or understand, your teacher can help you with them. You will find a lot of *fine* language in this extract, but not a lot that is really difficult. And the best way of finding out how things ought to go is to get on and have a shot at *doing* the play.

One way of arranging things is to divide your class into two groups, and have each group perform the sequence to the other, on different occasions. By casting the play twice over like this, it should be possible for everybody to take part. Certainly it will be necessary for everbody in each group to lend a hand in one way or another, as everybody lent a hand in Shakepeare's company. If there are about fifteen people in your group, it will be only *slightly* smaller than the group of people who acted the play for the very first time: and your production may resemble the way in which the play was originally performed in other ways too. Everything that you learn together from doing this play will stand you in good stead for trying *Hamlet* later: although that is a different kind of play, you will find that you can bring its story alive in the same way, if you work carefully together.

Appendix B

Greenwich Young People's Theatre

AIMS

The Youth Theatre and the Bowsprit Company work through educational drama. Educational drama aims not merely to provide a theatrical experience but to stimulate an awareness of life which leads to understanding and tolerance.

By using a range of stimuli from 'tag' games to intense emotional improvisation the young person is encouraged to develop a concept of learning through imagined experience. In this, it is important that the work is a logical extension of the social reality and the imaginative potential of both the individual and the group.

By working in a group, trusting and being trusted with the group, using but not relying upon the group, and then by individual expression, not only is the imagination developed but there also emerges an awareness of the mental and physical potential of the individual. A theatrical experience is one way of tying up the ends of an educational drama project.

One of the main problems in educational drama is that of imposition. It is essential that the actor-teacher is always the catalyst for the ideas of the young person and does not impose his own ideas in any way.

Educational drama, therefore, is a simple, practical aid to both formal and informal education, to both curricular and extra-curricular subjects. It leads to an awareness and understanding of the interrelationships of the individual and the group, of the individual and society.

BOWSPRIT COMPANY

The Bowsprit Company has established itself over the past two years as an important Theatre and Education Company working mainly in South-East and East London schools but also making valuable contacts in Kent and Essex schools. It supplies a great demand for presentations which are complementary to normal syllabus work.

One of the main problems facing the Company has been the problem of whether to do a performance themselves for the children, or whether the end result of a programme should be an equally balanced and totally integrated contribution from both Company and children. This has now been resolved and the Company now generally goes into schools for a whole day with a teaching session in the morning which builds up to a performance in the afternoon. In the morning session stories are worked out, situations are improvised, dances and songs are used and simple props are made. The afternoon performance is based entirely on the morning's work and further groups of children are involved. The children's involvement is very important at every level of the presentation.

The Company attempts to relate its work to projects already being carried out in the school and in some cases the Bowsprit presentation is the starting point for a new project. Further exploration of a theme is given impetus by an art teacher who works with the Company in a visually creative way, either visiting schools the day after each presentation, or working with the Company on the same day.

The Company often returns to the same schools and by doing so is building a good working relationship with teachers and pupils and establishing a framework within which educational drama can flourish successfully.

CLASSROOM TO THEATRE

The Greenwich Theatre, as a community theatre, feels that it is important to establish strong links with, and provide programmes for, local and other schools and colleges. As the Theatre and Education group of the Greenwich Theatre, the Bowsprit Company has held meetings with teachers at the theatre and with their support and contribution of ideas has provided courses which relate to the school curriculum and the Greenwich Theatre's productions. The Bowsprit Company hopes to extend this work in the future to cover not only curriculum, but also non-syllabus plays.

'MACBETH' COURSE (HELD IN THE THEATRE)

The *Macbeth* course aimed at illuminating certain aspects of the text through dramatic improvisation. In the theatre auditorium it was possible to demonstrate how lighting, set, sound effects and costume can be manipulated to achieve maximum effect in a production and the children were encouraged to participate in this.

Children's comments:

'. . . I thought the morning course was very well done and presented a good picture of *Macbeth*. It was good to know a few facts about the play and its history. The shortened version shown in the morning, lasting about three minutes, helped you to remember previously important events read in school.'

'. . . the way that the actors compared some of the scenes and thoughts to everyday life was very clever especially as a couple of the ideas were suggestions from the audience. It was also a good idea to act a scene from the play, starting from scratch and showing the audience the different views you have to look at before it is nearly perfect. . . .'

'. . . I thought I would write a few lines to show my appreciation of yesterday's explanatory session of the play *Macbeth*. To me the morning course has proved to be most helpful in my understanding of the play. . . .'

YOUTH THEATRE

Greenwich Youth Theatre was started in 1966 by Ewan Hooper as part of his concept of a community theatre in South-East London. It began its work under the auspices of Woolwich Recreational Institute but in July 1969 acquired its own premises – a disused church in Burrage Road, Plumstead. The building has a great potential as an arts centre for young people, but because of severe financial difficulties the plans for converting the church into a suitable centre have not, as yet, got under way. However drama classes have gone on despite cold and uncomfortable conditions.

Drama forms the largest part of the activities of the Youth Theatre – but in addition, music, environmental art, set construction and theatre wardrobe sessions are developing. A very active film group meets on Friday night and on Saturday morning a drama, art and music workshop is held for juniors. A folk club is held once a month and discotheques are organised on Saturday evenings. During the school holidays drama workshops are organised for local school children and groups from play centres in South-East London.

All the Youth Theatre's drama work is based on improvisation, although a performance is often aimed at in the case of the older groups. Sometimes ideas are developed in improvisation so that they crystallise into an 'understood script', sometimes a script is written based on improvisation.

At other times a scripted play is taken, its themes and character relationships worked on through improvisations and only during the last month or so is the script returned to. The Youth Theatre's work is aimed at providing drama activities that are a source of enjoyment, teamwork and 'group consciousness'.

The Youth Theatre in addition to its activities at Burrage Road, organises drama classes for juniors in the local community centres. Its long-term aim, however, is a building which will not only provide a drama and arts environment for the whole of South-East London, but which will also relate very specifically to the recreational needs of the community.

WORKOUT

Jon Walton's 'fourteen plus' drama group have been working on a presentation called *Drood*. This is based on Shakespeare's *Measure for Measure*, the story of a permissive society that has become corrupt and in which a man obtains power to re-establish law and order only to reveal and excercise his own brutality.

A member of the class explains how the ideas for *Drood* evolved: 'The themes and character relationship which Shakespeare portrayed were put in modern settings and parallels in a series of improvisations. In one, the idealistic, permissive society of the hippy was portrayed after some of its ideals had become tarnished.'

In another improvisation the sense of community and 'oneness' of drop-outs in a disused house was created. From there, the themes of brutality and authority coupled with a sense of alienation from other members of the group were developed with an almost frightening impact... the group began to identify with the attitudes and essential relationships arising from *Measure for Measure* and a greater understanding of the characters was arrived at.

Using the improvised work as a basis, the script and the musical score of *Drood* evolved and the final presentation is, therefore, a creation of the work of the group and not an imposition on the group.

Appendix C

The Emergent Africa Game*

In the autumn of 1970 a drama specialist from Ghana, Frances Ankma-Sey, was seconded to us. Then we came across *State of Emergency* by Dennis Guerrier and Joan Richards which was described as a 'programmed novel'. The authors had taken the problems of emergent African states and invented a composite state, 'Lakoto'. At each stage, the reader was invited to choose what he would do as prime minister. Here was the basic research for a drama game, and we used the characters and situations in *State of Emergency* as the basis for audience participation.

The project toured schools playing to 4th, 5th and 6th forms. The audience was between 100 and 120 and the session lasted half a day. The audience are sitting in a horse shoe round a playing area backed by a rear-projection screen. The Stage Manager introduces herself. 'Could you govern a country? We invite you to find out.' Independence Day. The Princess presents a parliamentary mace, the symbol of democracy from the Mother of Parliaments at Westminster to the Prime Minister, Okobo. The Union Jack is replaced by the new flag of Lakoto.

What are this country's chances? The Stage Manager summons a British reporter, Clare Furnival, who outlines Lakoto's geography and history. It is composed of two tribes, the majority peasant tribe, the Cantarbis and the merchant class, the Mokans. Clare interviews the Prime Minister, Okobo, a democrat educated in England, founder of the Centre Party. She meets Karome, the leader of the Cantarbi Nationalists, at a street demonstration. Lakoto's problems have just begun.

First cabinet meeting. What is to be the new nation's first priority? A Mokan merchant makes out a case for using their financial resources to recruit *experts from abroad* to start developing agriculture and industry at once. Karome disagrees violently, the priority should be the peasants in the shanty town. They need a welfare service to cope with the problems of unemployment. Another Cantarbi argues that the priority should be *education*, basic literacy, otherwise the people will never break away from ignorance and superstition. Already the cabinet is split.

* Belgrade Theatre, Coventry, Theatre in Education Company: report by Stuart Bennett on a secondary project (for pupils aged 14–18) in which the audience play roles in a simulated situation (Autumn 1970).

The Stage Manager intervenes and turns to the audience. Which course of action would you support if you were prime minister?

The audience divides into groups of twelve to fifteen. The actors act as discussion leaders. With some pupils the issues have to be explained again, but perhaps someone supports one alternative and stimulates an argument. After ten minutes the actors return from the audience and the stage manager takes a vote to see which course of action they approve of. Each group compares its opinions with others. What does Okobo support? He outlines the arguments as he sees them. He needs to find a role as mediator and a priority to unite his people. He chooses education. Time will tell if he has chosen wisely.

Clare visits a hydro-electric scheme and the audience share in a subsequent cabinet decision about the use of basic resources. Then we meet General Nashur. He believes in strong government. If the democratic cabinet system fails to govern effectively, it will be the duty of the army to restore law and order and take control. The sole member of the Lakoto Secret Service reports this to Okobo. Nashur has done nothing openly treasonable but we know his opinions. The M.I.5 agent recommends that General Nashur should be the victim of a convenient accident. The Stage Manager intervenes; Okobo can condone political assassination to safeguard democracy or wait for Nashur to move and arrest him for treason, or send him on a diplomatic mission abroad.

The audience discuss in groups the advisability and morality of the issue. Most pupils vote for assassination. Their response may have been superficial or they may be facing the reality of the situation with a positive act. Okobo cannot accept this. He sends Nashur abroad. Is he weak or honourable?

Clare hears of riots in a border town Benallahi. She drives there to investigate. A series of projected slides show us the type of town and the riots. Clare is accidentally killed. We have lost our guide and must go there ourselves.

The audience each take a scarf which is either red or green from the back of their seat, divide into two groups and move to separate working spaces. Two parallel drama sessions enable the pupils to take on the roles of the Cantarbi and Mokan rioters in a town where better jobs are held by the Mokans. Because of the riots the factories close and there is no work. Both groups in their roles converge on the playing area which becomes the market place. Karome arrives from the capital. The audience is now involved in an improvisation. He asks for details of their troubles and puts forward his solution – partition, Cantarbis to the east, Mokans to the west. The people may greet this with approval or reject it.

He is challenged by a man in a combat jacket. 'The root of your problems is not tribal hate but poverty. Forget your tribes, combine together, let us take over the factories and run them ourselves.' The pupils know enough to see the alternatives, though they may not be able to name them. They may not have previously taken any interest in politics. Now they are exploring partition and Castro-style socialism, but not theoretcally, they are on their feet in a drama situation. The man in the combat jacket is Ngami. He appeals for all those who will reject tribalism and join the workers combine to throw down their tribal scarves. Red and green scarves pile up. Some pupils won't join, they are suspicious of his motives, they don't trust him.

The Stage Manager stops the action. She gives Ngami a sten gun. Will he use force to maintain a popular movement? Ngami pauses. Some of his supporters are unsure. He decides – Yes. Those who resist us will be executed. Ngami stands for revolutionary action, not the slow process of democracy. The audience return to their seats discussing Ngami's decision. They revert to being an audience.

The actors play out the results of the rebellion. Okobo must decide whether to crush a popular movement caused by discontent over social conditions. Was he right to put education as his first priority? While he hesitates General Nashur acts. The M.I.5 agent assassinates him (unknown to Okobo) in order to prevent a military coup. Was Okobo right to refuse this course of action earlier? A neighbouring state, Mokoran, plans to annexe part of Lakoto under the pretext of protecting her investments. Okobo appeals successfully to the United Nations, and achieves a breathing space.

The Stage Manager interrupts the action. Three men have the ability to govern Lakoto. Okobo the democrat, Ngami the Marxist revolutionary Karome the partitionist. Which one is right?

This programme worked successfully for senior pupils of all ability levels. Different issues emerged each time it was played. Finally it was presented in our Studio Theatre for schools during the day and the general public in the evening.

The Bristol Street Theatre Troupe: A do-it-yourself kit

The Bristol Street Theatre Troupe was set up for three reasons: to entertain children free, to involve them in dramatic situations which they might continue later for themselves, and to publicise the Free Schools Association who sponsored the venture. It was hoped that children who saw and took part in our street plays would go on to create plays of their own in the Free Schools (holiday schools run by parents, students and other volunteers). We never actually continued our work by going into the Free Schools when the weekend of performances was over but since then a number of children have joined the group who had found us by seeing one of those first performances. The rest of the group is made up of teachers, school, university and college students in roughly equal proportions – some twenty-five people in all. We now meet twice a week to rehearse – once in a 'studio' in the University Dept of Education and once in the back room of a pub in an area where children and adults from various community centres can reach us more easily.

These 'rehearsals' consist of a rather odd mixture of different types of improvisation – that is to say, they would appear odd to any professional or student of drama. We use any method that helps to break down barriers and which contributes to the development of an actable story. To begin with it is not at all necessary for commitment to any theme, but once the theme is decided, things begin to move faster. Events in the calendar often decide the theme in advance – Hallowe'en and Guy Fawkes Night for example.

Types of improvisation: children's playground or party games – chasing, hiding, pretending to be animals. Or we might use movement – heavy or graceful – and start to build on to this basis elements of characterisation – grotesque heavy movements, haughty graceful movements. This leads into fuller characterisation and, in smaller groups of four or five, simple stories emerge. The haughty, sophisticated nobleman confronted with fat, grotesque peasant and two or more other characters – a tax collector, a witch, a fairy queen – all work together until their interaction produces a situation which develops into a story, which then can be told to the other groups, then re-enacted. A third type begins with the placing of two chairs in the centre of the room. After a pause someone will get up and go and sit in one of the chairs. What he or she chooses to do then to some extent determines what follows but in a large group there is no telling how the scene will end, as, one by one, individuals join the scene in the centre with some contribution of their own. As superintendent of a park, one week, (having stepped in to settle a dispute between an old lady and a tramp) you might find yourself having to cope with a request from an entrepreneur wanting to hold an open air pop festival. Some elements have to be put in consciously in an attempt to meet the demands of getting an audience together – processions, announcements, opening with a 'public event': an execution, a proclamation, a royal visit, the unveiling of a statue. We have always thought in terms of a 'stage' – a raised area with some kind of backing to it – from which excursions could be mad into direct physical involvement with children watching. These excu ons too had to be inserted deliberately in the plot as an essential element in the art of involving the children in the action. Our ideal was – often by Xmas pantomime methods – to make the kids feel they were controlling the action themselves. Our improvisation led to confrontations of opposites, of types – good and bad, beautiful and ugly. We decided it would be useful to take our types from the current vocabulary of young children – folk heroes, TV heroes, cinema heroes: Dracula, Guy Fawkes, Dr Who, Robin Hood. For the first play an idea was stolen from the fairy-tale of the princess who couldn't laugh and this was developed into the main theme of the story. Ideas quickly flowed – in improvisation and sitdown discussion – from this simple beginning: there could be an actual 'Sense of Humour' to find. It had to be stolen first – by Count Dracula (who else?). Other heroes were called to the rescue. Tarzan and Flash Gordon escaped (owing to the low average of the participants present) but Doctor Who and the composite/compromise (Aqua-Supa-Batman) with his accompanying chant 'AQUA*AQUA*SUPA*BATTY*BATTY*BATMAN!!!*' were quickly drafted into the plot. In half an hour, four weeks after weekly sessions had begun, a simple story-line had evolved and a couple of hours of improvisation in the acting through of that story-line produced what was clearly a performable 'play'. This could be broken down into scenes and each scene worked on separately. Progress accelerated on this once everyone had this scenario firmly fixed in their minds, so that they knew when to come on and towards what point to encourage each scene to move.

The feeling is rather like that of being one of a group that has shared the same experience – witnessing a crime or a natural disaster – and of the group's trying to tell what exactly took place. Each member of the group has the same facts to convey; when the member speaking hesitates, another immediately springs in to take up the story where he left off.

Though we now had a 'performable' play it was by no means ready for performance. It was undisciplined, long-winded, and at times too many people were talking at once. As soon as we began to rehearse in the open air all these problems were solved. And simply because it is an effort to make what you say audible in the street you know it's no use speaking before someone else has finished, because, if you do, neither of you will be heard; the urge to make long soliloquies soon dies and what were long drawn-out scenes in indoor improvisation are soon down to brief inter-changes of a dozen lines or so. The need to speak all lines directly 'out front', to shout 'key' lines, and to respond to advice and comment from the audience also influence the development of the 'play'.

At the end of all this we were left with the following scenario: Audience reaction/interaction/participation/control.

'Make the Queen Laugh'

1. Procession – singing while Dracula and his Monster guard the stage and gather a crowd there. Also three clowns play games with children.
2. Queen and entourage mount the stage (lorry). She starts to cry. The Prime Minister proclaims there will be a contest to make the Queen laugh, there is no prize but if you fail the penalty is death.
3. Numerous children mount the lorry to try and make the Queen laugh. They are sentenced to death for their failure* – as are three clowns who appear.
4. Dracula enters to make arrangements for the purchase (from the P.M.) for the severed heads for his monster.
5. Enter a messenger to say there is a man at the door – a doctor. 'Oh, who?' asks the P.M. 'That's right' replies the messenger. The children clarify the mystery and
6. call for Dr Who to enter. If the children protest that he isn't the real Dr Who he explains that he's changed appearance again. He asks what's the trouble. He says they're going about it the wrong way: 'Got to be scientific.' He draws a diagram of the Queen's head on the blackboard – four parts

The part which makes her angry	The part which makes her kind
The part which makes her cry	ʎddɐɥ ɹǝɥ sǝʞɐɯ ɥɔᴉɥʍ ʇɹɐd ǝɥꞱ

* The children to be instantly reprieved!

The fourth part is clearly at fault. He suggests an operation. P.M. exits saying he can't stand the sight of blood, mention of which substance prompts the entrance of Dracula: 'Did someone say blood?'

7. Dr Who's silly nurse helps him put on his 'Zoning gloves' which prevent him from being affected by the parts as he touches them. He takes parts out of the Queen's head having cut the top off with a saw ('You'll just feel a little saw') and the ladies in waiting take them from him, becoming angry, sad or kind according to which part they get and take the parts to show the children who likewise. . . . While Dr Who is setting up his pocket computer Dracula sneaks up and steals the faulty sense of humour: 'Now she'll never laugh again.'

8. P.M. comes back to check on outcome of the operation. Who says there's no panic and starts putting the three remaining parts of the brain back in the Queen's head. P.M. asks the children what's really happened. Only one man can help now, admits Dr Who, and that's AQUA*AQUA*SUPA*BATTY*BATTY*BATMAN. This chant is repeated with special hand movements until ASB arrives.

9. ASB has the situation explained to him (useful recap. for kids). He is left to catch Dracula. He happens to have his Dracula-disintegrator with him but it only works if there is 'a background hiss in the atmosphere'. The kids oblige. Dracula appears above the backing of the lorry – kids hiss. Chase. ASB chases Dracula towards the P.M. who makes the sign of the cross ('I read that in a book') and Dracula dies appropriately.

10. All that now remains is to get the Sense of Humour from Dracula's pocket, cure it and give it back to the Queen. But Dracula's monster is guarding it. Who says the monster can be tamed with a weed called 'Kindness' which grows in the area and he goes off with a group of children to look for some. Meanwhile the P.M. asks the remaining children to try hypnotism.

11. Who returns with 'Kindness' which is sprinkled over the now hypnotised monster. 'We love you monster, oh yes, we do.' The monster wakes up and is kind. The nurse asks can she have it as a pet. P.M. takes Sense of Humour out of Dracula's pocket.

12. Dr Who needs someone to operate on the S of H – an experienced brain surgeon. From the many who offer their services he selects one and together they cure the S of H – with sweets ('Anyone else here feeling sad?' – lots get cured with same medicine). The child goes off with the nurse to put the S of H back in the Queen's head. (She had retired to rest at the end of section 8.)

13. Meanwhile Dr Who and his group ('The Who') sing 'Talking about my O-o-operation':

People try to put her down
Just because she wears a frown
Things she does seem awful cold
But she won't die before she gets old
Not with my operation. . . .

14. The Queen and entourage return. When the child brain surgeon removes the Queen's veil we see she is smiling and cured. The Queen makes a speech: 'There will be Free Schools throughout the city.'
15. Final procession with songs.

RECREATION

We experienced varying reactions to our performances in different parts of the city. There was a marked contrast between playing in the adventure playground of St Paul's and Montpelier (central Bristol) and on the other sites where the restraining influence of parents was felt. In St Paul's there was no inhibition – and the usual actor/audience relationship was rarely in evidence. People who were afraid of Dracula were genuinely afraid. People who wanted to help the Queen genuinely wanted to help and brought her bouquets of wild flowers and packets of sweets. Most accepted our 'off-stage' convention and would carry on conversations only with those characters who were 'on'. Others, however, would think nothing of casually strolling into the thick of a mêlée between Dracula and the Prime Minister, untuning the latter's mandolin, trying on his hat and putting the boot into Dracula to help the proceedings move along. Others, again, became fully involved in the events and were eager to participate as allies of characters – regardless of whether they were 'on' or 'off'. So some kids saw the play from the point of view of one side only and would go behind the lorry to attend to the Queen, when she went off, occasionally reporting back to her events that were taking place 'on stage' and urging her to do something about it with real concern. At the Sunday market we were heckled by a group of 'skinheads' who were hostile to us because of the hairy student-like appearance of some of our number and because of the fact that we didn't appear to be making any money out of our work, an admission they just couldn't understand. Anyway, we ended up involving them too – thanks to a bit of improvisation from Count Dracula: 'My monster eats heads . . . *human* heads – with as little hair on them as possible.'

These performances were easy to handle with their continuous to and fro of suggestions making it seem as though we were spectator and that *they* were creating the drama which resulted from our interaction. In areas such as the Downs and the parks we had an 'audience', and they only responded when called upon to do so – green grass, sunshine, fresh air and, as said above, the occasional parent, all contributing to this. But still no inhibition: Dozens of volunteers for the talent contest, for the search for the plant called 'Kindness', for the brain operation and, at one park in a heavily populated area, over a hundred people joined our opening procession and joined the fifty who had gathered around the lorry while we were away. In these circumstances the play, which may seem to some readers to have been over-formulated and thus too rigid, did in fact change a lot. This is what makes street theatre such an exhilarating way of working with kids – for them and the performer. We aim to hold the interest and imaginations of the people we gather, snowball-like, from the streets. If we ever fail in this we'll have no one to blame, no scapegoat, but ourselves.

SCENARIOS

'Guy Fawkes'

1. While the King, Queen, Soldiers and 'Guy Fawkes' (as a stuffed dummy) make a procession, the witches teach children around the lorry various games which will help them to trick the King's soldiers and avoid paying them any money, e.g. turning into animals when approached.

2. The procession returns and the two soldiers mount the stage hoisting the 'dummy' with them (more soldiers were sometimes recruited from the kids). The soldiers say the King and Queen will be arriving shortly and need money. The dummy they say, is an example of what happened to one chap who refused. The soldiers go to get the King.

3. The 'dummy' slowly wakes up and tells the children his story. He says he wants to get his own back on the King and asks the children to wake him up if an opportunity arises.

4. The soldiers return with the King and Queen. A stormy reception awaits them from the children who by this time are very hostile. The King demands more money for his supersonic galleon and for marmalade for the Queen's breakfast (etc.), and sends the soldiers to get it. Animal noises are heard all around as the soldiers demand money. They return empty-handed. The King suspects witchcraft and orders the soldiers to arrest a witch.

5. A fleeing witch runs straight into the King and knocks him and the Queen over. Eventually she is tied to the stake and matches are produced. She protests that she will do anything for her freedom. She can change things with magic. One of the soldiers asks to be turned into Georgie Best. With the help of a chant from the

* The second scenario was created and formed by the Bristol Street Theatre Troupe.

children this is done. So the King asks if she can make gold out of stone. She says she can but must be left alone. The King and Queen go leaving sentries at the 'door'.

6. She calls all the other witches to help, confessing that witches can't make gold. They plan instead to conjure up some conspirators to kill the King. They hide (off the lorry) when the spell begins to work.

7. Three conspirators emerge from the cauldron. They think they're in a bank under which they have been tunnelling. At sight of the children and the witches they realise they have gone wrong and are scared but list their criminal credentials ('How many banks have you robbed?' 'Well, this was to be our first, I done a bubblegum machine though.') The witches ask them who their leader is – each points to another. 'We might as well have a stuffed dummy'. Which prompts a few kids to shout 'Guy Fawkes' but failing this G.F. very quietly says 'What about me?'

8. The conspirators drag the 'dummy' forward and wake him up. He asks the kids if this is his chance to get his own back. 'Will I be famous?' But if he is to be famous he'll need a name. The children shout 'Guy Fawkes'. He inspects the criminals who are to be his gang. They've no discipline. Some kids are asked to show them how to stand to attention. Then they all go off to look for explosives.

9. The King returns for his gold. Finding none he throws the witches into jail: 'Put them behind bars.' A set of bars is brought on and the witches are put behind it and pushed to one side of the lorry. Soldiers and King leave.

10. Guy and his men return with a bomb but can't find the witches. The children point out where they are. Guy says he'll free them when he's planted the bomb. They work out how to get to the House of Commons. They ask for suggestions for a password, then set off.

11. Meanwhile a soldier sets a barrel on the lorry and announces: 'The cellars of the Houses of Parliament.' The conspirators enter stealthily muttering the password. They suddenly notice a stranger has slipped in amongst them. He doesn't know the password. He's the caretaker – Big Ben. ('That rings a bell.') What are they doing there? 'Planting a bomb,' says the fat conspirator. 'A flower,' corrects Guy. The caretaker suggests a suitable spot for planting it and they overpower, tie and gag him. They plant the bomb and while the men take out the fuse (it is several yards long and goes through all the children). Guy goes off to free the witches.

12. At which point the King and Queen enter, slightly drunk, looking for their vintage wine, which is kept in the cellars. They call the caretaker – find him, ungag him and hear his story. A soldier defuses the bomb and the King suggest a firework could be put in its place

to fool the conspirators. Then all hide, the caretaker being left there so there'll be no suspicion.

13. Guy and his men return. They take pity on the caretaker and free him. Guy orders his men to light the fuse. They do so. 'You fools, you've lit the wrong end.' They all throw themselves to the floor. The firework fizzles.

14. Enter the King (actually somewhere to the side of the stage): 'Arrest that man!' Guy is arrested, his men escape. He is tied to the stake and given a last request. He asks for a cigarette. He is told they're not good for his health but as he's about to go up in smoke anyway. ... He sneezes so much that all the matches lit for his cigarette by the two soldiers are blown out. They go off to get the King and Queen and some more matches.

15. The witches return (earlier they reassure the kids around them that Guy will be safe as otherwise the kids would rescue Guy themselves). They free Guy Fawkes, putting a dummy in his place.

16. King, Queen, Soldiers return and tell the people that hard times are ahead and that Guy Fawkes is going to be made an example of. Then they find the dummy. The King therefore proclaims that from now on bonfires will be lit every year and stuffed dummies burned so that one year 'we'll get the *real* Guy Fawkes and I'll be rid of him for ever'. The King and Queen exit to a stream of abuse from their by now most unloyal not to say revolutionary subjects and the witches return with the conspirators and Guy to celebrate their victory in song and dance.

'St George and the Dragon'*

1. Four *dwarves* dance with children then climb on to the lorry/platform to ask if anyone has seen their three lost brothers. St George arrives to ask if anyone has seen his girl friend, Cinderella. He gives the *dwarves* a ring which matches one Cinderella has, so that if they see her they can summon him by putting the rings together.

2. When St George has gone mechanical men arrive singing 'We are mechanical men, we serve our master'. Their master is the Dragon who announces that everyone is his slave and must work for him in his money mines. He offers them transistors, washing machines, etc. (Balloons with these words written on are handed out). The *dwarves* eagerly accept to work for the Dragon and are led off by the mechanical men.

* Third production of the Bristol Street Theatre Troupe performed for Human Rights Day (10 December) at a meeting of Human Rights groups and in the shopping area of Bristol on the 12 December. Also performed at other sites in Bristol 12–13 December and in the Old England public house.

3. St George comes on in search of Merlin, whom he summons with a chant (M.E.R.L.I.N.). Merlin searches in his beard for Cinderella's whereabouts and sees she has been captured by the Dragon. He gives George a gadget to defuse the mechanical men. George sings his song: 'I kill Dragons'.

4. The *dwarves* return exhausted and miserable after work in the mines. They demand tea. A girl is brought on by a mechanical man and she tells them there is no tea, no transistors, no washing machines, and no escape. They tell her about George who can kill Dragons. She says she is Cinderella his girl friend and gives them her ring, as the mechanical men and Dragon come to take her away and order the *dwarves* back to work.

5. They summon St George with the rings and he says he will kill the Dragon. The *dwarves* go on strike (singing 'We shall not be moved') and the Dragon returns angrily as George sings 'We'll kill the Dragon'.

6. St George gives the Dragon sword and shield and they fight. The Dragon is killed (or sometimes spared, having managed to get out the line 'Peter Scott would never forgive you').

7. But then three mechanical men return. St George defuses them with Merlin's gadget. A 'technical genius' from the audience of kids is required to take off the heads of the now dead men. This is done and it is found that inside are the three lost *dwarves*. Merlin is summoned to restore them to life, which he does by means of a long fat stick raised in front of each dwarf/robot to a vertical position. The *dwarves* celebrate but George is anxious about Cinderella. Merlin brings her forward and offers her and George the entire treasure accumulated by the Dragon. Protesting that it is not the Dragon's money but the *dwarves'*, who worked for it, and that money only causes trouble anyway, George has Merlin change the gold into chocolate and they distribute it among the Dragon's former 'slaves'.

ORGANISATION

Costumes. Free loan from local rep. or make simply out of old curtains, egg boxes.

Scenery: It shouldn't be necessary to have much in the way of scenery but some form of back-drop is needed to concentrate attention and to provide an 'off-stage' area. It has to be firmly secured and waterproof. Borrow (local TV stations use vast quantity of harboard flats; local amateurs clearing stock) and secure with ropes and tent pegs.

Props. Make. The help of local art students was enlisted for the parts of the brain and the Dracula disintegrator.

Sites. Adventure playgrounds, youth centres, parks markets, open spaces in housing estates and places people go on Sunday afternoons. This should be planned so the local press, etc. can publish times and places.

Permission: parks, etc. – Parks Dept of the Corporation, housing estates – Housing Dept or Engineer's Dept; other Corporation departments may control specific sites. Approach through the City Public Relations Office which, in our case, handled all further negotiations with other departments. Permission usually involves guarantees to be made by the group that litter will be cleared and 'grass areas reinstated'. Sometimes restrictions are made on the use of amplification equipment and on the taking of a collection. We also perform at an open-air Sunday market which pays us to do so, thus helping to finance cost of making the above, etc. The police should be notified of times and places in advance, and they will want assurance that children watching the performances are not in danger from passing traffic and that pavements are not obstructed. The Fire Chief showed some interest at first, but discovering we had no entrances, exits, gangways, usherettes or toilets and no electrical apparatus saw little point in trying to enforce the Theatres Act or in issuing a licence. The only proviso was that we didn't practise hypnotism – a promise we weren't entirely faithful to (see scenario)!

This article originally appeared in *New Theatre Magazine*, Volume XI No. 1, published by the Department of Drama at Bristol University.

Bibliography

The compilation of a bibliography is a complex undertaking, particularly liable to error and omission. This alphabetical index has been assembled from the author's personal library, recommendations of colleagues, the scanning of professional journals and a search of the appropriate categories of the B.N.B. from 1965 onwards.

Whilst the list does not claim to be exhaustive, it is hoped that it will be helpful in at least three ways. Firstly, it is intended as a directory for teachers looking for additional literature in a particular area of drama or a related subject. Secondly, it might be helpful to school and college librarians seeking to enlarge their drama and theatre sections, and thirdly, it might be a useful reference for students wanting to build up their own library of books.

The categories do not accord to any specific bibliographical system, but have been devised from an anlysis of the titles available. The books range from the exclusively academic, through teaching techniques to books for children. Full details are given in this index of books referred to in the text or commented upon at the close of the individual sections. The reference is usually to the latest edition of the text and only limited mention is made of books that are out of print.

Acting
Boleslavsky, Richard, *Acting: The First Six Lessons* (Dobson, London, 1949).
Cole, Toby, *A Handbook of the Stanislavski Method*. (Bonanza Books, N.Y., 1970).
Guthrie, Tyrone, *Acting* (Studio Vista, London, 1971).
Hayman, Ronald, *Techniques of Acting* (Methuen, London, 1969).
McGaw, Charles, *Acting is Believing* (Holt, Rinehart & Winson, N.Y., 1965).
Mackenzie, Frances, *The Amateur Actor* (Garnet Miller, London, 1967).
Marowitz, Charles, *The Method as Means* (Jenkins, London, 1961).
Moore, Sonia, *The Stanislavski System* (Gollancz, London, 1966).
Oxenford, Lyn, *Playing Period Plays* (Garnet Miller, London, 1970).
Redgrave, Michael, *The Actor's Ways and Means* (Heinemann, London, 1966).
Stanislavski, Constantin, *Building A Character* (Reinhardt, London, 1950).
Stanislavski, Constantin, *Creating a Role* (New English Library, London, 1968).

Amateur Theatre
Burton, Peter and Lane, John, *New Directions* (MacGibbon & Kee, London, 1970).

Newton, Robert, *A Creative Approach to Amateur Theatre* (Garnet Miller, London, 1967).
Rendle, Adrian, *Everyman and His Theatre* (Pitman, London, 1968).
Wykes, Alan, *The Handbook of Amateur Dramatics* (Barker, London, 1966).

Art
Langer, Susanne, *Feeling and Form* (R. & K.P., London, 1953).

Melzi, Kay, *Art in the Primary School* (Blackwell, Oxford, 1967).
Read, Herbert, *Education Through Art* (Faber, London, 1958).
Sausmarez, Maurice de, *Basic Design* (Studio Vista, London, 1964).

Commedia dell' Arte
Oreglia, Giacomo, *The Commedia dell' Arte* (Methuen, London, 1968).

Costume
Berk, Barbara, *The First Book of Stage Costume and Make-Up* (Ward, London, 1966).
Brooke, Iris, *Medieval Theatre Costume* (Black, London, 1967).
Geen, Michael, *Theatrical Costume and the Amateur Stage* (Arco, London, 1968).
Green, Ruth, *The Wearing of Costume* (Pitman, London, 1966).
Jackson, Sheila, *Simple Stage Costumes and How to Make Them* (Studio Vista, London, 1968).
Laver, James, *Costume Through the Ages* (Thames & Hudson, London, 1963).
Laver, James, *A Concise History of Costume* (Thames & Hudson, London, 1969).
Peters, Joan and Sutcliffe, Anna, *Making Costume for School Plays* (Batsford, London, 1971).
Snook, Barbara, *Costumes for School Plays* (Batsford, London, 1965).
Tompkins, Julia, *Stage Costumes and How To Make Them* (Pitman, London, 1969).
Truman, Nevil, *Historic Costuming* (Pitman, London, 1969).

Creative Dramatics
Siks, G. B., *Creative Dramatics: An Art for Children* (Harper & Row, N.Y., 1958).
Siks, G. B., and Dunnington, H. B., *Children's Theatre and Creative Dramatics* (Univ. of Washington, Seattle, 1961).

Criticism and Analysis
Bear, Bernard de (ed.), *Varieties of Dramatic Experience* (Univ. of London Press, London, 1969).
Bentley, Eric, *The Life of Drama* (Methuen, London, 1965).
Boulton, Marjorie, *The Anatomy of Drama*, R. & K.P., London, 1968).
Brooks, Cleanth and Heilman, Robert, *Understanding Drama* (Holt, Rinehart & Winston, N.Y., 1945).
Brown, John Russell, *Drama* (Heinemann, London, 1968).
Corrigan, Robert, *Theatre in the Twentieth Century* (Spectrum, N.Y., 1969).
Dawson, S. W., *Drama and the Dramatic* (Methuen, London, 1970).
Esslin, Martin, *The Theatre of the Absurd* (Eyre & Spottiswoode, London, 1962).
Grotowski, J., *Towards a Poor Theatre* (Methuen, London, 1969).
Styan, J. L., *The Elements of Drama* (Cambridge U.P., London, 1960).
Wells, Stanley, *Literature and Drama* (R. & K. P., London, 1971).

Dance (see also *Movement*)
Bruce, Violet and Tooke, Joan, *Lord of the Dance* (Pergamon, Oxford, 1966).
Carroll, Jean and Lofthouse, Peter, *Creative Dance for Boys* (Macdonald & Evans, London, 1969).

Laban, Rudolf (rev. L. Ullman), *Modern Educational Dance* (Macdonald & Evans, London, 1964).

Lofthouse, Peter, *Dance: Activity in the Primary School* (Heinemann, London, 1970).

Preston-Dunlop, Valerie, *Handbook for Modern Educational Dance* (Macdonald and Evans, London, 1963).

Russell, Joan, *Dance in the Primary School* (Macdonald & Evans, London, 1965).

Russell, Joan, *Creative Dance in the Secondary School* (Macdonald & Evans, London, 1969).

Winearls, Jane, *Modern Dance* (Black, London, 1968).

Dance Drama

Bruce, Violet, *Dance and Dance Drama in Education* (Pergamon, Oxford, 1966).

Design and Construction (Stage)

Chilver, Peter and Jones, Eric, *Designing a School Play* (Batsford, London, 1968).

Corey, Irene, *The Mask of Reality* (Anchorage Press, Kentucky, 1968).

Jones, Eric, *Stage Construction for School Plays* (Batsford, London, 1969).

Joseph, Stephen, *Scene Painting and Design* (Pitman, London, 1964).

Library Association, *Stagecraft and the Theatre* (London Library Assn, 1965).

Napier, Frank, *Curtains for Stage Settings* (Garnet Miller, London, 1949).

Rowell, Kenneth, *Stage Design* (Studio Vista, London, 1968).

Warre, Michael, *Designing and Making Stage Scenery* (Studio Vista, London, 1966).

Directories

A Directory of Drama Adjudicators (Guild of Drama Adjudicators, London).

French's *Books on Acting, the Theatre, Cinema and Television* (London).

French's *The Guide to Selecting Plays*, in 5 Parts (London).

Henshaw, David, 'A Bibliography of Dance and Related Arts', *Laban Art of Movement Magazine* (May 1971).

Stacey, Ron (ed.), *Theatre Directory* (*Amateur Stage* Handbook).

Stacey, Ron (ed.), *A Classified Guide to Play Selection* (*Amateur Stage* Handbook).

Drama Studios

Courtney, Richard, *The Drama Studio* (Pitman, London, 1967).

Dept. of Education and Science, *Drama and Music* (H.M.S.O., London, 1966).

English

Burton, E. J., *Teaching English Through Self Expression* (Evans, London, 1967(rep.)).

Cook, Elizabeth, *The Ordinary and the Fabulous* (C.U.P., London, 1969).

Fowler, R. S. and Dick, A. B. J., *English 11/12, 12/13, 13/14, 14/15, 15/16,* (Allen & Unwin, London, 1971–3).

Hodgson, John and Richards, Ernest, *Living Expression* (Ginn, London, 1968–70).

Parry, Christopher, *English Through Drama* (C.U.P., London, 1972).

Thompson, Denys, *New Directions in the Teaching of English* (C.U.P., London, 1972).
Whitehead, Frank, *The Disappearing Dais* (Chatto & Windus, London, 1966).

Fights and Weapons
Blackmore, H. L., *Arms and Armour* (Studio Vista, London, 1964).
Hobbs, William, *Techniques of the Stage Fight* (Studio Vista, London, 1967).
Moncreiffe, I. and Pottinger, D., *Simple Heraldry* (Nelson, London, 1953).
Wise, Arthur, *Weapons in the Theatre* (Longman, London, 1968).

General Theories
Alington, A. F., *Drama and Education* (Blackwell, Oxford, 1961).
Bolton, Gavin, 'Drama and Theatre in Education', *Drama and Theatre in Education*, ed. Dodd and Hickson (Heinemann, London, 1971).
Burton, E. J., *Drama in Schools* (Jenkins, London, 1964).
Coggin, Philip, *Drama in Education* (Thames & Hudson, London, 1956).
Cook, Caldwell, *The Play Way* (Heinemann, London, 1917).
Courtney, Richard, *Play, Drama, and Thought* (Cassell, London, 1968).
Dept. of Education and Science, *Drama: Education Survey 2* (H.M.S.O., London, 1968).
Dodd, Nigel and Hickson, Winifred (eds.), *Drama and Theatre in Education* (Heinemann, London, 1971).
Heathcote, Dorothy, 'Drama and Education: Subject or System', *Drama and Education*, ed. Dodd and Hickson (Heinemann, London, 1971).
Piaget, Jean, *Play, Dreams and Imitation in Childhood* (R. & K.P., London, 1962).
Slade, Peter, *Experience of Spontaneity* (Longman, London, 1968).
Slade, Peter, *An Introduction to Child Drama* (Univ. of London Press, London, 1969).
Way, Brian, *Development Through Drama* (Longman, London, 1967).

'Games'
Walford, Rex, *Games in Geography* (Longman, London, 1969).

Improvisation
Chilver, Peter, *Improvised Drama* (Batsford, London, 1967).
Hodgson, John and Richards, Ernest, *Improvisation* (Methuen, London, 1967).
Pickering, Kenneth, *Drama Improvised* (Garnet Miller, London, 1971).
Spolin, Viola, *Improvisation for the Theatre* (North Western U.P., 1963).

Lighting
Bentham, Frederick, *The Art of Stage Lighting* (Pitman, London, 1968).
Ost, Geoffrey, *Stage Lighting* (Jenkins, London, 1954).

Linguistics
Crystal, David, *Linguistics* (Penguin, Harmondsworth, 1971).

Make-up
Blore, Richard, *Stage Make-Up* (Stacey Pubns, Bromley, Kent, 1965).
Jones, Eric, *Make-Up for School Plays* (Batsford, London, 1969).
Melvill, Harold, *Magic of Make-Up* (Barrie & Rockliff, London, 1966).
Perrotet, Philippe, *Practical Stage Make-Up* (Studio Vista, London, 1967).
Stanley, Adrian, *Guide to Greasepaint* (French, London).

Masks
Grater, Michael, *Paper Faces* (Mills & Boon, London, 1967).
Green, Michael, *Space Age Puppets and Masks* (Harrap, London, 1969).

Mime
Bruford, Rose, *Teaching Mime* (Methuen, London, 1958).
Gray, Vera and Percival, Rachel, *Music, Movement and Mime for Children* (Oxford U.P., London, 1966).

Movement (see also *Dance*)
Bruce, Violet, *Movement in Silence and Sound* (Bell, London, 1970).
Cameron, McD and M., *Education and Movement in the Infant School* (Blackwell, Oxford, 1969).
Collins, S., *Practical Modern Educational Dance* (Macdonald & Evans, London, 1969).
I.L.E.A., *Movement Education for Infants* (County Hall, London, 1965).
Jordan, Diana, *Childhood and Movement* (Blackwell, Oxford, 1966).
Laban, Rudolf, *Mastery of Movement* (Macdonald & Evans, London, 1950).
Morris, Margaret, *My Life in Movement* (Owen, London, 1969).
Oxenford, Lyn, *Design for Movement* (Garnet Miller, London, 1964).
Sherbourne, Veronica, 'Movement in Preparation for Drama', *Drama and Theatre in Education*, ed. Dodd and Hickson (Heinemann, London, 1971).

Music
Dept of Education and Science, *Drama and Music* (H.M.S.O., London, 1966).
Driver, Ann, *Music and Movement* (O.U.P., London, 1936).
Eele, M. and Davies, L., *Carols for Acting* (Novello, London).
Jarvis, M. A., *Musical Games for Infants* (Faber, London, 1951).
Jarvis, M. A., *Dances and Musical Activities for Juniors* (Faber, London, 1951).
Paynter, John, *Sound and Silence* (C.U.P., London, 1970).
Thackray, R. M., *Playing for Dance* (Novello, London, 1963).
Wilson, M., *Movement Through Song* (O.U.P., London, 1962).

Play-making
Barr, Enid, *From Story into Drama* (Heinemann, London, 1964).
Cobby, Maisie, *The Playmakers* (Pitman, London, 1951).
Cornwell, Paul, *Creative Playmaking in the Primary School* (Chatto & Windus, London, 1970).
Haggerty, Joan, *Please, Miss, Can I Play God?* (Methuen, London, 1966).

Play Production and Direction
Allen, John, *Play Production* (Dennis Dobson, London, 1950).
Fernald, John, *The Play Produced* (Deane, London).
Fernald, John, *Sense of Direction* (Secker & Warburg, London, 1968).
Marowitz and Trussler, *Theatre at Work* (Methuen, London, 1967).
National Federation of W.I, *Focus on Drama* (W.I. Pubns, London, 1968).
Nuttall, K., *Play Production for Young People* (Faber, London, 1963).
Roose-Evans, James, *Directing a Play* (Studio Vista, London, 1968).
Slater, Derek, *Plays in Action* (Pergamon, Oxford, 1964).
Stanislavski, K., *Stanislavski on the Art of the Stage* (Faber, London, 1967).
Sterne, R. L., *John Gielgud Directs Richard Burton in 'Hamlet'* (Heinemann, London, 1968).

Poetry

Anderson, Margaret, *Splendour of Earth* (George Philip, London, 1954).
Guildhall School of Music and Drama, London, *Anthology of Poetry, Prose and Play Scenes* (London, annually).
Hourd, Marjorie, *Education of the Poetic Spirit* (Heinemann, London, 1949).
Morris, Helen, *Where's That Poem?* (Blackwell, Oxford, 1967).
Woodland, Esme, *Poems for Movement* (Evans, London, 1966).

Punch and Judy

Fraser, Peter, *Punch and Judy* (Batsford, London, 1968).
Speaight, George, *Punch and Judy* (Studio Vista, London, 1970).

Puppets

Bainbridge, Cecil, *Hand Puppets* (Museum Press, London, 1968).
Beresford, Margaret, *How to Make Puppets and Teach Puppetry* (Mills & Boon, London, 1966).
Binyon, Helen, *Puppetry Today* (Studio Vista, London, 1966).
Currell, David, *Puppetry in the Primary School* (Batsford, London, 1970).
Fraser, Peter, *Introducing Puppetry* (Batsford, London, 1968).
Green, Michael, *Space-Age Puppets and Masks* (Harrap, London, 1969).
Lanchester, Waldo, *Hand Puppets and String Puppets* (Dryad, Leicester, 1969).
Philpott, Alexis, *Eight Plays for Hand Puppets* (Miller, London, 1968).

Religious Education

Allen, Arthur, *Religious Drama for Amateur Players* (Faber, London, 1958).
Bruce, Violet and Tooke, Joan, *Lord of the Dance* (Pergamon, Oxford, 1966).
Love, Margaret, *Let's Dramatise* (Nat. Christian Ed. Council, Nutfield, 1968).
Peachment, B., *The Defiant Ones* (Religious Ed. Press, Oxford, 1969).

School Play

Courtney, Richard, *The School Play* (Cassell, London, 1966).

Shadowgraphs

Hawkesworth, Eric, *Making a Shadowgraph Show* (Faber, London, 1969).
Reiniger, Lotte, *Shadow Theatres and Shadow Films* (Batsford, London, 1970).

Shakespeare

Hodges, C. Walter, *The Globe Restored*, 2nd edn (O.U.P., London, 1968).
Hodges, C. Walter, *Shakespeare and the Players*, 2nd edn (Bell, London, 1970).
Hudson, A. K., *Shakespeare and the Classroom*, 2nd edn (Heinemann, London, 1963).

Speech

Bruford, Rose, *Speech and Drama* (Methuen, London, 1948).
Burniston, C., *Speech for Life* (Pergamon, Oxford, 1966).
Casciani, J. W., *Speak for Yourselves* (Harrap, London, 1966).
Chilver, Peter, *Talking* (Batsford, London, 1968).
Colson, Greta, *Voice Production and Speech* (Museum Press, London, 1963).
Colson, Greta, *Speech Practice*, 2nd edn (Museum Press, London, 1970).
Crump, Geoffrey, *A Manual of English Speech* (Dobson, London, 1966).
Harvey, Basil, *The Scope of Oracy* (Pergamon, Oxford, 1968).

Hodgson, John and Richards, Ernest, *Living Expression* (Ginn, London, 1968–70).

Horner, A. Musgrave, *Movement, Voice and Speech* (Methuen, London, 1970).

Jones, Daniel, *An Outline of English Phonetics*, 8th edn (Heffer, Cambridge, 1957).

Morgan, Diana, *Living Speech in the Primary School* (Longman, London, 1966).

Piaget, Jean, *Language and Thought of the Child* (R. & K.P., London, 1959).

Reeves, James and Culpan, Norman, *Dialogue and Drama* (Heinemann, London, 1950).

Turner, Clifford, *Voice and Speech in the Theatre* (Pitman, London, 1950).

Wise, Arthur, *Talking Together* (Harrap, London, 1968).

Wise, Arthur, *Your Speech* (Longman, London, 1968).

Wise, Arthur, *Spoken English for C.S.E.* (Harrap, London, 1966).

Stage Management

Baker, Hendrik, *Stage Management and Theatrecraft* (Garnet Miller, London, 1969).

Chilver, Peter, *Staging the School Play* (Batsford, London, 1967).

Napier, Frank, *Noises Off* (Miller, London, 1962).

Simulation

Boocock, S. S. and Schild, E. (eds), *Simulation Games in Learning* (Sage, Beverley Hills, Calif., 1968).

Tansey, P. J. (ed.), *Education Aspects of Simulation* (McGraw Hill, N.Y., 1971).

Walford, R. and Taylor, J. L., *Simulation in the Classroom* (Penguin, Harmondsworth, 1972).

Walford, Rex, 'Games and Simulations', *New Movements in the Study and Teaching of Geography*, ed. N. J. Graves (Temple Smith, N.Y., 1972).

Teaching Techniques and Approaches
General

Bruford, Rose, *Speech and Drama* (Methuen, London, 1948).

Collins, Freda, *Children in the Market Place* (Garnet Miller, London, 1968).

Courtney, Richard, *Teaching Drama* (Cassell, London, 1965).

Parry, Christopher, *The Mummery* (Chatto & Windus, London, 1967).

Pemberton-Billing, R. N. and Clegg, J. D., *Teaching Drama* (Univ. of London, London, 1968).

Ranger, Paul, *Experiments in Drama* (Univ. of London, London, 1971).

Walker, Brenda, *Teaching Creative Drama* (Batsford, London, 1970).

Infant

Gray, Vera and Percival, Rachel, *Music, Movement and Mime for Children* (O.U.P., London, 1966).

James, Ronald, *Infant Drama* (Nelson, London, 1967).

Lutley, Phyllis, *Teaching with a Purpose* (Educational Drama Assn, 1968).

McCrea, Lilian, *Stories to Play in the Infant School* (O.U.P., London, 1959).

Primary

Casciani, J. W. and Watts, Ida, *Drama in the Primary School* (Nelson, London, 1966).

Cobby, Maisie and Newton, Eric, *The Playmakers* (Pitman, London, 1951).

Goodridge, Janet, *Drama in the Primary School* (Heinemann, London, 1970).
Lowndes, Betty, *Movement and Drama in the Primary School* (Batsford, London, 1970).
Morgan, Elizabeth, *A Practical Guide to Drama in the Primary School* (Ward Lock, London, 1968).
Martin, William and Vallins, Gordon, *Exploration Drama* (Evans, London, 1968).

Secondary
Adland, D. E., *The Group Approach to Drama* (Longman, London, 1969).
Barnfield, Gabriel, *Creative Drama in Schools* (Macmillan, London, 1968).
Cobby, Maisie, *Calling All Playmakers* (Pitman, London, 1956).
Hudson, John and Slade, Peter, *A Chance for Everyone* (Cassell, London, 1967).
King, Colin, *A Space on the Floor* (Ward Lock, London, 1972).
Payne, Philip, *Legend and Drama* (Ginn, London, 1968).

Television and Radio
BBC, *Using Radio and Television: A Guide to Classroom Practice* (BBC Pubns, London, 1969).
BBC, *School Radio and the Tape Recorder* (BBC Pubns, London).
Maclean, Roderick, *Television in Education* (Methuen, London, 1968).

Theatre History
Brown, Ivor, *Look at Theatres* (Panther, London, 1969).
Burton, E. J., *Student's Guide to World Theatre* (Jenkins, London, 1962).
Burton, E. J., *Student's Guide to British Theatre* (Jenkins, London, 1964).
Gascoigne, Bamber, *World Theatre* (Ebury Press, London, 1968).
Hartnoll, Phyllis, *A Concise History of the Theatre* (Thames & Hudson, London, 1968).
Hartnoll, Phyllis, *The Oxford Companion to the Theatre* (O.U.P., London, 1967).
Joseph, Stephen, *New Theatre Forms* (Pitman, London, 1968).
Male, David, *The Story of the Theatre*, 2nd edn (Black, London, 1967).
Nicoll, Allardyce, *The Development of the Theatre*, 5th edn (Harrap, London, 1966).
Peach, L. du Garde, *The Story of the Theatre* (Wills & Hepworth, Loughborough, 1970).
Priestley, J. B., *The Wonderful World of the Theatre* (Macdonald, London, 1969).
Robinson, Ruth, *The Theatre* (Oliver & Boyd, Edinburgh, 1968).
Roose-Evans, James, *Experimental Theatre from Stanislavski to Today* (Studio Vista, London, 1970).
Southern, Richard, *The Seven Ages of the Theatre*, 2nd edn (Faber, London, 1968).
Taylor, Alison, *The Story of the English Stage* (Pergamon, Oxford, 1967).
Taylor, John Russell, *The Penguin Dictionary of the Theatre* (Penguin, Harmondsworth, 1966).

Youth Theatre
Courtney, Richard, *Drama for Youth* (Pitman, London, 1964).

Leach, Robert, *Theatre for Youth* (Pergamon, Oxford, 1970).
Masters, Simon, *The National Youth Theatre* (Longman, London, 1969).
Nuttall, Kenneth, *Play Production for Young People* (Faber, London, 1963).
Taylor, Alison, *Off Stage and On* (Pergamon, Oxford, 1969).
Arts Council, *The Provision of Theatre for Young People in Great Britain* (London, 1968).

Index